Tendin
A Financi

for

Agricultural Families

Navigating Dementia

by

Keith C. Piscitello, CFP®

ISBN: 979-8-234-01120-6

Preface

This book helps farmers and ranchers navigate the complex tax, legal, financial, and caregiving challenges of a dementia diagnosis to protect their land, fund quality care, and ensure their legacy passes successfully to the next generation.

This material is intended solely for educational and informational purposes. It is not intended to provide—and should not be relied upon as—legal, tax, medical, accounting, or individualized financial advice. Readers should consult qualified professionals, including attorneys, tax advisors, medical professionals, and licensed financial professionals, regarding their specific circumstances.

Nothing in this book constitutes
a recommendation regarding any, product, strategy, or financial plan or a solicitation for any advisory, brokerage, legal, or tax service.

Any strategies, concepts, or examples described are illustrative only and may not be appropriate for all individuals.

Examples, scenarios, projections, or references to potential tax outcomes, asset protection strategies, or estate planning techniques are hypothetical. They do not represent actual or future results. Statistics or third-party data referenced are believed to be reliable but cannot be guaranteed. protection strategies, or estate planning techniques are hypothetical. They do not represent actual or future results. Statistics or third-party data referenced are believed to be reliable but cannot be guaranteed.

Keith is a Registered Representative of and offers securities through Cambridge Investment Research, Inc., a broker/dealer, member FINRA/SIPC and advisory services through Cambridge Investment Research Advisors, Inc., a Registered Investment Adviser. Cambridge and Simply Sophisticated Wealth Planning LLC are not affiliated.

Table of Contents:

1.	When the Diagnosis Comes to the Farm	9
2.	The First 90 Days: Critical Decisions That Protect Your Land and Livelihood	17
3.	Who's Minding the Ranch? Legal Authority and Decision-Making Documents	33
4.	The True Cost of Care: Funding Options That Don't Force a Fire-Sale	47
5.	Protecting the Land: Estate Planning Strategies for Multi-Generational Farms	63
6.	Tax Landmines and Opportunities: Preserving Wealth Through the Transition	79
7.	Medicare, Medicaid and the Farm: Navigating Healthcare Benefits Without Losing Everything	97
8.	Preparing the Next Generation: Succession Planning When Time is Short	115
9.	Building Your Care Team: Coordinating Medical, Legal, and Financial Advisors	131

10.	From Crisis to Confidence: Your 12-month Action Plan	151
	Appendix: Your Action Tracker	171
	Endnotes and References	173
	Additional Resources and Data Sources	179
	Disclaimers	183

Chapter 1: When the Diagnosis Comes to the Farm

You've noticed the signs for months, maybe longer. Your spouse forgot to close the gate—something they've done thousands of times without thinking. They got confused about which field was planted with what. They asked you the same question three times in one morning. You told yourself it was just stress, or age, or too many long days in the sun.

Then came the appointment. The tests. The words that changed everything: Alzheimer's disease. Or maybe it was vascular dementia, or Lewy body dementia. The specific diagnosis almost doesn't matter in that moment, because what you heard was this: *everything is about to change.*

And here's the thing nobody tells you when you're sitting in that doctor's office—when you're a farmer or rancher, dementia doesn't just affect your family. It affects your operation, your livelihood, your legacy, and the land itself.

You're Not Alone

If you're reading this, you're part of a growing community. Research shows that 42% of Americans over age 55 will eventually develop dementia, and agricultural families face even greater risks. The reasons aren't hard to understand. Our farming population is aging—the average age of American farmers is now approaching 60. Many of us have spent decades exposed to pesticides, herbicides, and other chemicals that research is increasingly linking to cognitive decline.

Studies show that agricultural workers have 46% greater odds of developing dementia compared to those in other occupations, and the contributing factors are significant. Chronic exposure to organophosphate and organochloride pesticides has been linked to lasting toxic effects on the central nervous system. Noise-induced hearing loss from farm equipment—recognized as a major dementia risk factor—is more common among agricultural workers than in other occupations. Depression, which doubles the risk of developing dementia, occurs at higher rates among farmers due to longer work hours, isolation, financial pressures, and pesticide exposure itself.

And unlike folks in town who might work a desk job until 65 and then retire, farmers often work well into their 70s and

80s, managing complex operations that require split-second decisions, detailed record-keeping, and constant adaptation to weather, markets, and regulations.

When dementia enters the picture, it doesn't just affect whether you remember where you put your keys. It affects whether you can manage payroll, negotiate grain contracts, make decisions about livestock sales, or know when to trust your judgment on a major equipment purchase.

The Weight You're Carrying

Right now, you might be feeling overwhelmed. Maybe you're angry—at the diagnosis, at the timing, at the unfairness of it all. You've worked your whole life to build something, to be a good steward of the land, to create something you could pass on. And now there's this shadow over everything.

You're probably worried about things that other people don't even think about. How do you keep the operation running when the person who's managed it for 40 years can't trust their own memory? What happens to the farm if you need to pay for care? The financial burden is staggering—in 2025, the total cost of dementia care in the United States reached $781 billion, with families and friends providing $247 billion in unpaid care alone. The average annual cost per person with dementia is over

$53,000, and lifetime costs can exceed $321,000. For farming families where wealth is tied up in land and equipment rather than liquid assets, these numbers are especially daunting.

Can you afford professional caregiving without selling land that's been in the family for generations? Who's going to make medical decisions if you can't? And the question that probably keeps you up at night: will your kids be able to keep this place, or will everything you've built be lost to medical bills and taxes?

These aren't small concerns. They're real, legitimate fears about your family's future and your legacy.

But here's what I want you to know: you have more options than you think you do. And the fact that you're reading this book right now—that you're willing to face this challenge head-on—means you're already doing something that will make a tremendous difference for your family.

Why This Is Different

Dementia planning for farm and ranch families isn't like planning for anyone else. Most financial planning books talk about 401(k)s and IRAs. They assume your wealth is liquid, that you can just write a check when you need to pay for care. They don't understand that your "wealth" is tied up in land, equipment, livestock, and growing crops. They don't get that you can't just stop working because you have a diagnosis—the cows still need feeding, the fields still need tending, and the bank still expects that loan payment.

Your situation is also complicated by the fact that many farm assets have appreciated enormously over the years. That land your grandfather bought for $500 an acre might be worth $10,000 an acre now. That's wonderful for your net worth on paper, but it creates massive tax implications if you need to sell or transfer assets to qualify for benefits or pay for care.

And then there's the emotional side. For many farming families, the land isn't just an asset—it's identity, heritage, and purpose all rolled into one. The thought of losing it, or seeing it pass out of the family, can feel like losing a part of yourself.

What This Book Will Do for You

Over the next several chapters, we're going to walk through the key areas you need to address to protect your farm, fund quality care, and ensure your legacy continues:

Legal protection and decision-making authority. We'll talk about the documents you need in place *right now*—powers of attorney, healthcare directives, and trust structures that protect both you and your operation when cognitive decline makes it impossible to manage everything yourself.

Funding care without losing the farm. We'll explore creative strategies for paying for care that don't require selling the land, including long-term care insurance, Medicaid planning that protects agricultural assets, veterans benefits, and other resources you might not know about.

Tax planning that preserves wealth. We'll look at the specific tax challenges farm families face and strategies to minimize the bite when assets need to be transferred or liquidated.

Succession planning when time is short. Even if you didn't plan for this, we'll discuss ways to prepare the next generation to take over, including training, gradual transitions, and legal structures that make succession smoother.

Building and coordinating your care team. You'll learn how to assemble the right professionals—attorneys, financial advisors, geriatric care managers, and medical providers—and get them working together instead of in silos.

Throughout this book, you'll find practical checklists, real-world examples from families who've navigated this journey, and clear action steps you can take immediately.

Moving Forward

The diagnosis has been made. You can't change that. But what you do in the weeks and months ahead will determine whether this disease dismantles everything you've built or whether your family navigates it with dignity, security, and confidence about the future.

The land has always required tending—through droughts and floods, through good markets and bad, through every challenge that came your way. Now it's time to tend what matters most: your family's security, your own dignity, and the legacy you'll leave behind.

Let's get to work.

Chapter 2: The First 90 Days: Critical Decisions That Protect Your Land and Livelihood

The days after a dementia diagnosis can feel like you're moving through fog. There's grief to process, family conversations to have, and a thousand questions swirling in your head. But there's also a window of opportunity that won't stay open forever.

In the first 90 days after diagnosis, while cognitive abilities are still relatively intact, you have the chance to make decisions and put protections in place that might become impossible—or at least much more complicated—down the road. Think of this period like spring planting: miss your window, and you're fighting an uphill battle all season long.

Why the Clock Is Ticking

Here's something most people don't understand about dementia and legal capacity: you don't need to be completely incapacitated before you lose the ability to make certain legal decisions. Different legal documents require different levels of mental capacity, and once that capacity is questioned, everything becomes harder.

Right now, if your spouse or parent received the diagnosis, they can likely still sign legal documents, make informed decisions, and express their wishes clearly. Six months from now? A year from now? That might not be true. And if you wait until capacity is clearly diminished, you may find yourself in probate court asking a judge for guardianship—a process that's expensive, time-consuming, emotionally draining, and often avoidable with proper planning.

I've seen too many farming families wait, thinking they had more time. They meant to get the paperwork done. They planned to have those conversations. Then one day they needed to refinance the farm loan or sell a piece of equipment, and the banker or attorney said, "I'm sorry, but I don't think they have capacity to sign this." At that point, your options narrow considerably.

The Immediate Actions That Buy You Time

Let's talk about what needs to happen in these first 90 days. This isn't about having everything figured out—it's about creating the legal and financial framework that will give you flexibility as the disease progresses.

Get the Legal Documents in Order—Now

If you don't have current powers of attorney, healthcare directives, and a will or trust, this is your top priority. Not next month. Now.

A durable power of attorney for finances allows your designated agent (usually a spouse or adult child) to manage financial matters if the person with dementia can't. This includes everything from paying bills to managing bank accounts to making decisions about the farm operation. Without it, you may need a court-appointed conservatorship just to access accounts or sell assets.

A healthcare power of attorney (sometimes called a healthcare proxy) designates who makes medical decisions. When doctors start asking whether to pursue aggressive treatment or how to manage care, you need clear legal authority to speak on your loved one's behalf.

An advance directive or living will spells out wishes for end-of-life care. These conversations are never easy, but having them now—while the person with dementia can clearly express their values and preferences—is a gift to the family members who will eventually need to make those decisions.

For farm families, you also need to consider whether a revocable living trust makes sense. A trust can hold farm assets and allow for seamless management if the person who created it becomes incapacitated. It also avoids probate, which can be crucial if you need to act quickly to keep the operation running.

More about getting your legal documents in order in Chapter 3: Who's Minding the Ranch?

Establish Decision-Making Authority for the Farm

Here's where it gets specific to agricultural operations. You need clarity about who can make operational decisions about the farm or ranch. This might mean:

- Adding authorized signers to business bank accounts
- Updating signature authority on operating loans and lines of credit
- Clarifying roles if you have a family farming partnership or LLC
- Ensuring the person taking over daily management has legal authority to enter contracts, buy and sell livestock, negotiate with vendors, and make operational decisions

Many farm operations run informally—Mom and Dad have always just handled things together. But when one person's capacity diminishes, that informal arrangement can become a legal nightmare. Your banker, your feed supplier, your equipment dealer—they all need to know who has authority to act on behalf of the operation.

Have the Honest Family Conversation

This is probably the hardest part of the first 90 days, and it's something no legal document can do for you. You need to gather the family—especially adult children who might be involved in the farm's future—and have an honest conversation about what's happening and what it means.

These conversations should cover:

- The diagnosis and what to expect as the disease progresses
- Who will take on additional responsibilities in the farm operation
- What the long-term plan is for the farm (succession, sale, lease)
- How care decisions will be made and who's responsible for what

- Financial realities—what resources are available and what the care might cost

Yes, it's uncomfortable. Yes, there might be disagreements or hurt feelings. But I promise you: having this conversation now, when everyone's head is clearer, is far better than trying to hash it out in a crisis six months from now.

Do a Financial Inventory

You need a clear picture of where you stand financially. This means gathering:

- All bank and investment account statements
- Loan documents and current balances
- Insurance policies (life, health, long-term care, crop, liability)
- Property deeds and titles
- Lists of equipment, livestock, and other farm assets
- Recent tax returns (at least three years)
- Information about any pensions, Social Security, or veteran's benefits

This inventory serves two purposes. First, it helps you understand what resources you have available for care.

Second, it creates a roadmap for the person who'll be managing finances going forward.

Many farm couples have operated for decades with one person handling "the books" and the other focused on field work or livestock. If the person who managed the money is the one with dementia—or if the healthy spouse needs to suddenly take over financial management—this inventory becomes absolutely critical.

Review Insurance Coverage

Long-term care insurance, if you have it, needs to be reviewed immediately. What does it cover? What's the daily benefit? What's the elimination period before benefits kick in? You need to understand these details now so you can plan accordingly.

If you don't have long-term care insurance, it's probably too late to get it (most policies won't cover pre-existing conditions like dementia). But you should still review your other coverage—health insurance, Medicare supplements, life insurance—to understand what protection you have and whether any policies have cash value or other features that might be useful.

Connect with Professional Advisors

You can't do this alone, and you shouldn't try. In the first 90 days, you need to start building your support team:

- An elder law attorney who understands Medicaid planning and farm asset protection
- A financial advisor with experience in agricultural estate planning
- A certified public accountant who knows farm taxation
- A geriatric care manager or social worker who can help navigate medical and care decisions

I know that for many farm families, bringing in "outsiders" feels unnecessary or even uncomfortable. You've always handled things yourself. But dementia planning for farm families is genuinely complex—it sits at the intersection of healthcare, elder law, tax planning, business succession, and agricultural finance. Very few people have expertise in all these areas, which is why you need a team.

What Happens If You're Already Past 90 Days?

Maybe you're reading this and thinking, "We got the diagnosis eight months ago. Did we miss our chance?"

The answer is no—but your options may be more limited. If the person with dementia still has capacity (even diminished capacity), many of these steps can still be taken. If capacity is truly gone, you'll need to explore alternatives like guardianship, joint ownership structures, or creative solutions with the assets you can still access.

The key is to act now with whatever options you still have. Don't let regret about lost time prevent you from protecting what you still can.

Looking Ahead

These first 90 days are about creating a foundation. You're putting legal protections in place, gathering information, building your team, and having crucial conversations. It won't solve every problem you'll face in the years ahead, but it will give you the tools and authority to make decisions when they're needed most.

In the next chapter, we'll dive deeper into the specific legal documents you need and what should be in them to protect farm assets and ensure your wishes are followed. But for now, focus on the immediate action items. The farm has taught you that preparation matters, that timing is everything, and that hoping for good weather isn't the same as planning for drought.

Time to put that wisdom to work.

Your First 90 Days Checklist

Use this checklist to organize and prioritize what needs to be addressed immediately after a dementia diagnosis:

Week 1-2: Legal Foundation

- ☐ Schedule appointment with elder law attorney to discuss powers of attorney and healthcare directives
- ☐ Gather existing legal documents (wills, trusts, deeds, business formation documents)
- ☐ Identify who will serve as agent/trustee for financial and healthcare decisions
- ☐ Review current business structure (sole proprietor, partnership, LLC) and decision-making authority

Week 2-4: Financial Inventory

- ☐ Compile list of all bank accounts, investment accounts, and retirement accounts
- ☐ Gather all loan documents (operating loans, equipment loans, land mortgages)
- ☐ List all insurance policies and contact information (health, life, long-term care, farm liability, crop)

- [ ] Collect property deeds, vehicle titles, and equipment titles
- [ ] Obtain last 3 years of tax returns (personal and business)
- [ ] Document current livestock inventory and major equipment

Week 3-5: Business Continuity

- [ ] Contact your banker to discuss signature authority on farm accounts and lines of credit
- [ ] Add authorized signers to business checking and operating accounts
- [ ] Notify key vendors and suppliers of any changes in who can authorize purchases
- [ ] Review and update operating agreements or partnership documents
- [ ] Document standard operating procedures for critical farm tasks

Week 4-6: Insurance and Benefits Review

- [ ] Review long-term care insurance policy (if applicable) and understand coverage details

- ☐ Contact Social Security Administration to discuss disability benefits if applicable
- ☐ Review Medicare or health insurance coverage and understand what's covered
- ☐ Check eligibility for VA benefits (if either spouse is a veteran)
- ☐ Review life insurance policies and consider whether to access cash value

Week 6-8: Family Communication

- ☐ Schedule family meeting with spouse, adult children, and other key stakeholders
- ☐ Discuss diagnosis, prognosis, and what to expect
- ☐ Clarify roles and responsibilities for farm management going forward
- ☐ Address succession planning intentions (even if preliminary)
- ☐ Document who's responsible for what (caregiving, operations, finances)

Week 8-10: Professional Team Building

- ☐ Schedule consultation with elder law attorney
- ☐ Meet with financial advisor experienced in agricultural planning
- ☐ Connect with accountant to discuss tax implications of potential asset transfers
- ☐ Identify geriatric care manager or social worker for care planning support
- ☐ Research local dementia support groups and caregiver resources

Week 10-12: Care Planning Basics

- ☐ Schedule follow-up appointment with neurologist or specialist
- ☐ Research local care options (adult day care, in-home care, memory care facilities)
- ☐ Begin rough estimates of care costs based on current diagnosis
- ☐ Consider home modifications that may be needed as disease progresses
- ☐ Discuss with family what "quality care" means and what the priorities are

Ongoing (Throughout First 90 Days)

- ☐ Keep detailed notes of conversations with doctors, attorneys, and advisors
- ☐ Create a binder or digital folder with all important documents
- ☐ Begin tracking monthly farm income and expenses if not already doing so
- ☐ Research dementia progression to understand what to expect
- ☐ Take care of yourself—identify respite care options and support for the caregiver

---

Note: This checklist is comprehensive but should be adapted to your specific situation. Not every item will apply to every farm family, and you may identify additional tasks specific to your operation. The goal is progress, not perfection. Start with what's most urgent for your situation and keep moving forward.

Chapter 3: Who's Minding the Ranch? Legal Authority and Decision-Making Documents

Every farmer knows you can't run a hundred head of cattle without fences. The fences don't stop the cattle from grazing—they just make sure the cattle graze where you want them to.

Legal documents work the same way. They're not about restricting your freedom or taking away control. They're about building the right fences so that when dementia starts pushing against the boundaries of what you can safely manage, there's a structure in place to protect you, your family, and your farm.

Without those fences? Chaos.

The Four Documents You Can't Farm Without

Think of these as the four corners of your pasture. Miss one, and everything can scatter.

1. Durable Power of Attorney for Finances

This is your financial quarterback. The person you name here can pay bills, manage bank accounts, file taxes, buy and sell property, and make business decisions on your behalf.

The word "durable" is critical. A regular power of attorney expires when you become incapacitated—exactly when you need it most. A durable power of attorney keeps working even after you can't.

For farm families, this document needs to be bulletproof. Your agent should have explicit authority to:

- Operate and manage the farm business
- Buy, sell, lease, or mortgage real estate
- Hire and fire employees
- Enter into contracts with suppliers and buyers
- Access safe deposit boxes and digital accounts
- Manage livestock and equipment sales
- Handle crop insurance claims and government program payments
- Create, amend, or revoke trusts if needed for Medicaid planning

Here's what most people get wrong: they create a power of attorney that's too vague. "Handle my financial affairs" sounds fine until your banker says they need specific language about operating loans, or your attorney says the POA doesn't give clear authority to do Medicaid planning.

Work with an attorney who understands agricultural operations. The $500 you spend now on a properly drafted POA can save you $50,000 in legal fees later trying to get a guardianship.

Key takeaway: A durable financial power of attorney is like having a spare set of keys to the tractor. You hope you never need them, but when you do, you need them to work perfectly.

2. Healthcare Power of Attorney

This document names who makes medical decisions when you can't. It's different from the financial POA because medical decisions require different judgment calls.

Your healthcare agent will make decisions about:

- What treatments to pursue or decline
- Which doctors and facilities to use
- Whether to try experimental treatments

- End-of-life care preferences
- Whether to move from home care to facility care

For farm families, there's often tension between the person best suited to manage the farm (usually someone with agricultural knowledge and business sense) and the person best suited to make healthcare decisions (often someone geographically close, emotionally equipped for medical discussions, and available for frequent appointments).

You don't have to name the same person for both roles. In fact, it's often better not to. The son who's taking over the farm operation may not be the daughter who lives 20 minutes from the hospital and has time to attend doctor appointments.

Key takeaway: Pick your healthcare agent based on who can be present, ask the right questions, and honor your wishes—not based on who knows the most about combines.

3. Living Will or Advance Directive

This is where you put your wishes in writing. Do you want to be kept alive on machines if there's no hope of recovery? Do you want aggressive treatment for every infection, or comfort care when the time comes?

These are hard questions. Nobody wants to think about them. But consider this: if you don't answer these questions now, your family will have to answer them for you—often while standing in a hospital hallway, exhausted and grief-stricken, with no idea what you would have wanted.

That's not fair to them, and it's not the legacy you want to leave.

Farm folks tend to be practical about life and death. You've helped birth calves and you've put down animals that were suffering. You understand that sometimes the kind thing to do is to let go. Put that wisdom on paper.

Key takeaway: A living will is your last gift to your family—clarity when they need it most.

4. Will or Revocable Living Trust

This is how your assets get distributed after you're gone. If you die without a will, state law decides who gets what—and state law doesn't care about your farm staying intact or your specific wishes for which kid gets which piece of land.

For many farm families, a revocable living trust makes more sense than a simple will. Here's why:

A trust avoids probate. Probate is a public court process that can take months or years, during which your farm assets might be frozen. If you've got crops in the ground, livestock to feed, or loan payments due, you can't afford to wait six months for a probate court to give your family access to operating funds.

A trust also provides for management if you become incapacitated. If you and your spouse are co-trustees, and one of you develops dementia, the other can keep managing everything seamlessly. If both of you become incapacitated, your successor trustee steps in without needing court approval.

Trusts are especially valuable when you have:

- Land in multiple states (avoiding probate in each state)
- Complicated family situations (blended families, estranged children)
- Significant assets that you want managed professionally
- Privacy concerns (trusts aren't public record like wills)

The downside? Trusts cost more upfront—typically $2,000 to $5,000 depending on complexity. But for a farm worth $2 million, that's a small investment for the protection and flexibility you get.

Key takeaway: A will says where things go after you're gone. A trust says where things go and who manages them if you can't. For farm families, that second part is often more important.

Getting the Names Right

The hardest part of these documents isn't the legal language—it's choosing who to name.

Some families have an obvious choice. One kid has been farming alongside you for 20 years, everyone trusts them, and they're capable of handling both the farm and the tough decisions.

But many families don't have that luxury. Maybe your kids aren't interested in farming. Maybe they're in different states with their own careers. Maybe there's tension between siblings, or you're worried about putting too much burden on one person.

Here are some strategies that work:

Name co-agents who must act together. This builds in accountability and shared responsibility. The downside is that both people have to agree on every decision, which can slow things down.

Name co-agents who can act independently. Either person can make decisions on their own. This is faster but requires high trust that they'll consult each other.

Name a primary agent with backups. Your first choice gets priority, but if they can't serve (because of distance, health, or other reasons), the next person steps in.

Divide responsibilities. One person handles farm operations, another handles personal finances, a third handles healthcare decisions. This distributes the load and uses each person's strengths.

Consider a corporate trustee. For families with significant assets or complicated dynamics, naming a bank or trust company as trustee can provide professional management and remove family conflict. You can name family members as co-trustees so they still have input.

Whatever you decide, have the conversation with the people you're naming. Don't surprise someone at your funeral by letting them discover they're responsible for a 500-acre farm and they have no idea where to start.

Key takeaway: Choosing agents isn't about playing favorites—it's about matching responsibilities to capabilities and keeping your farm running.

The Mistake That Costs Families Everything

Here's the scenario I see over and over:

Dad gets diagnosed with dementia. Mom is healthy and capable, so nobody worries too much. They have old powers of attorney from 15 years ago naming each other. Everything seems fine.

Two years later, Mom has a stroke. Suddenly both parents are incapacitated, and the old POAs only name each other—not the kids. Now the farm is frozen. Nobody can access accounts, make business decisions, or manage operations. The kids need to file for emergency guardianship, which takes weeks or months and costs tens of thousands of dollars.

Meanwhile, bills aren't getting paid. Livestock need care. The spring planting window is closing.

This nightmare is completely avoidable. Your legal documents need successor agents—the people who step in if your first choice can't serve. And those documents need to be current.

Legal documents aren't like cast-iron skillets—they don't last forever. Laws change. Family situations change. A POA from 1998 may not have the authority needed for today's digital banking and complex Medicaid planning.

Review your documents every 3-5 years, and update them whenever there's a major life change: marriage, divorce, birth, death, diagnosis, or change in business structure.

Key takeaway: Old legal documents are like old fence posts—they might look fine until you lean on them and they collapse. Check them regularly and replace them when needed.

What Happens Without These Documents

Let me paint you a picture of what happens when a farm family doesn't have proper legal documents in place.

Your spouse develops dementia and can no longer manage finances. You need to refinance the farm loan to take advantage of lower interest rates, but your spouse's signature is required and they can't legally sign documents anymore.

Without a power of attorney, you have two choices: file for guardianship (expensive, time-consuming, and requires proving your spouse is incompetent in court) or let the higher interest rate stand and lose thousands of dollars over the life of the loan.

Or this: Your parent is in the hospital with pneumonia, confused and unable to communicate their wishes. The doctor wants to know whether to intubate. Your siblings disagree on what to do. Without a healthcare power of attorney and living will, the hospital may default to the most aggressive treatment—even if your parent explicitly told you a hundred times they never wanted to be on machines.

Or this: Your spouse dies unexpectedly, and your jointly-owned farm goes into probate. For the next year, you can't sell land, refinance debt, or make major business decisions without court approval. The operating loan comes due and you can't negotiate an extension because you don't have clear legal authority. You might lose the farm not because of bad farming but because of bad paperwork.

These aren't hypothetical nightmares. These are real situations I've seen destroy farm families who thought they had more time.

Key takeaway: The fences you build with legal documents aren't there to restrict you—they're there to protect you when the storms come. And the storms always come.

Taking Action

If you're reading this and you don't have these documents in place, make the call today. Not next week. Not after harvest. Today.

If you have documents but they're more than five years old, pull them out and review them. Better yet, have an elder law attorney review them and tell you what needs updating.

Yes, this costs money. Expect to pay $1,500 to $4,000 for a comprehensive estate plan including all four key documents. For farm families with complex operations or significant assets, the cost might be higher.

But compare that cost to what you'll pay if you don't have these documents and something happens. Guardianship proceedings can cost $15,000 to $50,000. Probate for a farm can eat up 5-10% of the estate value. The cost of not being able to act quickly in a crisis? Potentially everything.

You insure your crops. You insure your buildings. You insure your equipment. These legal documents are insurance for your family's future. They're not optional—they're essential.

Key takeaway: You can pay an attorney a few thousand dollars now, or you can pay an attorney tens of thousands later. One protects your farm. The other dismantles it.

In the next chapter, we'll talk about the question that keeps farm families awake at night: how to pay for care without selling the land. But none of those strategies work without the legal foundation we've just built. First the fences, then the livestock.

Chapter 4: The True Cost of Care: Funding Options That Don't Force a Fire Sale

Let's talk about the elephant in the barn: money.

You can have all the legal documents in the world, but if you can't figure out how to pay for care without selling the farm, those documents just become instructions for how to dismantle everything you built.

The good news? There are more options than you think. The bad news? Most families don't know about them until it's too late to use them effectively.

What Care Actually Costs

First, let's get real about numbers. When people think about dementia care costs, they often picture the nursing home at the end. But the journey to that point costs money too—often lots of it.

Early stage dementia might mean hiring someone to help a few hours a week. That's $20-30 per hour, maybe $500-1,000 per month.

Middle stage might mean adult day care (around $1,500-2,000 per month) or part-time home care workers (easily $3,000-5,000 per month).

Late stage might mean full-time home care ($8,000-12,000 per month) or memory care facility ($6,000-10,000 per month depending on your location).

And these costs can stretch for years. The average person lives 4-8 years after an Alzheimer's diagnosis, but some live 20 years.

Do the math: even conservative estimates put total care costs at $200,000-400,000. For longer progressions or more intensive care needs, you're looking at $500,000 or more.

For a farm family with $2 million in net worth but only $50,000 in liquid assets, these numbers are devastating. You're land-rich and cash-poor, which is great for leaving a legacy but terrible for funding care.

Key takeaway: Dementia care isn't a one-time expense—it's a marathon that can drain six figures from your estate. Plan accordingly.

Strategy 1: Long-Term Care Insurance (If You Have It)

If you were smart enough to buy long-term care insurance before the diagnosis, congratulations. You're ahead of the game.

But you still need to understand what you have:

Daily benefit amount: Most policies pay a fixed amount per day, like $150 or $200. If your actual care costs $250 per day, you're covering the difference out of pocket.

Benefit period: Is it three years? Five years? Lifetime? When the policy runs out, you're self-funding.

Elimination period: This is like a deductible—you pay out of pocket for 30, 60, or 90 days before the insurance kicks in.

What's covered: Home care? Assisted living? Memory care? Adult day care? Not all policies cover all types of care.

Inflation protection: Policies without inflation riders become less valuable over time. A $150 daily benefit from 2005 doesn't go nearly as far in 2025.

Here's the part people miss: you need to file a claim and get approved. Don't wait until you're in crisis mode. As soon as the diagnosis is made and care needs are starting, contact your insurance company. Get the paperwork started. Understand what documentation they need from doctors.

Many families wait too long to file, then discover they've been paying out of pocket for months of care that would have been covered.

Key takeaway: Long-term care insurance is like crop insurance—it only helps if you file the claim properly and on time.

Strategy 2: Veterans Benefits

If you or your spouse served in the military, there are benefits available that most farming veterans don't know about.

Aid and Attendance: This VA benefit can provide up to $2,431 per month (2025 rates) for a veteran, $1,318 for a surviving spouse, or $2,893 for a couple. It's designed to help pay for in-home care or assisted living.

To qualify, you need:

- 90 days of active military service with at least one day during a wartime period
- An honorable discharge

- Limited income and assets (though the VA doesn't count your primary residence or farm operation)
- Need for assistance with daily activities

Here's where it gets interesting for farm families: the VA has generous asset exemptions for working farms. They understand that land and equipment are business assets, not available resources for care.

The application process is complicated and can take 6-12 months, so start early. Consider working with a VA-accredited attorney or veterans service officer who can help navigate the paperwork.

Key takeaway: Veterans benefits are like finding money in an old coat pocket—it's yours, you earned it, but you have to know to look for it.

Strategy 3: Medicaid (Yes, Even for Farm Families)

Most farmers hear "Medicaid" and think, "That's not for us. We have assets."

But Medicaid planning for farm families is different than for everyone else. The key is understanding which assets count and which don't.

Exempt assets (don't count toward Medicaid limits):

- Your primary residence (up to $713,000 in equity in some states, unlimited in others)
- One vehicle
- Personal belongings and household goods
- Property used in a trade or business (this is the big one for farmers)
- Certain prepaid funeral arrangements

That "trade or business" exemption can protect farmland, equipment, livestock, and other farm assets if they're legitimately part of an active operation. The farm doesn't have to be huge or highly profitable—it just needs to be real.

The catch: Someone needs to be actively operating the farm. If you shut down operations after the diagnosis, the assets may no longer qualify as exempt. This is why succession planning is critical—getting the next generation actively involved in operations before the diagnosis can protect the farm.

The five-year look-back: Medicaid examines all asset transfers made in the five years before you apply. Gifts, sales below market value, or asset transfers can trigger penalties that delay eligibility. This is why advance planning matters. Transfers made today may not affect Medicaid eligibility until five years from now.

Spousal protections: If one spouse needs nursing home care and the other is healthy, the healthy spouse can keep:

- The home
- One car
- About $157,920 in countable assets (2025 limit, varies by state)
- All income in their own name

This means the healthy spouse can continue living on the farm, collecting farm income, and maintaining the operation even while the sick spouse receives Medicaid-covered care.

Key takeaway: Medicaid is like a complicated grain contract—the rules seem impossible at first, but with the right advisor, you can make them work in your favor.

Strategy 4: Strategic Use of Trusts

This is where advance planning really pays off. Irrevocable trusts can protect assets from Medicaid's reach, but they need to be set up at least five years before you need care.

How it works: You transfer farm assets into an irrevocable trust. You give up ownership (important for Medicaid purposes) but can structure the trust so that:

- You continue receiving income from the farm
- You retain the right to live on the property
- You direct how the assets are managed
- The assets pass to your heirs without probate

After five years, these assets are protected from Medicaid's asset limits and estate recovery.

The trade-off: Once assets are in an irrevocable trust, you can't easily get them back out. This is permanent planning. You're betting that you'd rather protect the farm for the next generation than maintain flexibility to sell or refinance.

For farm families thinking about succession anyway, this can be a perfect fit. You're essentially formalizing the transfer to the next generation while protecting assets from long-term care costs.

Key takeaway: Irrevocable trusts are like planting an orchard—they take years to mature, but the harvest can be worth the wait.

Strategy 5: Caregiver Agreements

Here's an option that works beautifully for farm families where an adult child is willing and able to provide care: a formal caregiver agreement.

Instead of having your daughter quit her job to care for you "out of love," you pay her a fair market rate for caregiving services—typically $25-40 per hour depending on the level of care and your location.

Why this makes sense:

- Your daughter gets compensated for work she's actually doing
- The payments are income to her (she reports them on taxes) but not a gift for Medicaid purposes
- You're converting countable assets (cash) into exempt assets (payment for services)
- The arrangement is legal and above-board

The key details:

- It must be a written contract before care begins
- The pay rate must be reasonable for your area
- The caregiver must report the income
- You must actually pay for services rendered (not in advance)
- Keep detailed records of care provided

This strategy works especially well when the caregiver is already involved in the farm. They can provide care while continuing to help with operations, and the farm income can fund their caregiving compensation.

Key takeaway: A caregiver agreement turns family help into a legitimate business arrangement that protects assets and compensates the caregiver fairly.

Strategy 6: Life Insurance as a Funding Source

If you have cash value life insurance, you might be sitting on a hidden funding source.

Options include:

- Taking policy loans (borrowing against the cash value)

- Withdrawing cash value (may be partially tax-free)
- Surrendering the policy for its cash value
- Selling the policy to a third party (life settlement)

For farm families, life insurance can be especially valuable because it's liquid. When everything else is tied up in land and equipment, that $50,000 or $100,000 in life insurance cash value can fund the first year or two of care.

The downside: Using life insurance for care means less death benefit for your heirs. But if the choice is between funding care today or leaving a bigger inheritance tomorrow, care wins.

Consider this strategy for policies that aren't needed for estate planning or business continuation. Maybe you bought insurance 30 years ago when the kids were young and you were heavily in debt. If those needs are gone, the policy can serve a new purpose.

Key takeaway: Life insurance is like seed saved from last year's crop—you bought it for one purpose, but it can be replanted for another.

Strategy 7: Income from Farm Assets

Sometimes the best funding source is the one you already have: the farm itself.

If operations are continuing (either you're still working or the next generation has taken over), farm income can fund care. This might mean:

Leasing land: Cash rent from productive farmland can generate $150-300 per acre annually. A 200-acre lease could generate $30,000-60,000 per year.

Selling production: If livestock or crop operations are continuing, that income can be directed toward care costs.

Custom work: If you have equipment, renting it out or doing custom work for neighbors generates income without selling assets.

Timber or mineral rights: If your land has marketable timber or mineral rights, selective harvesting or leasing can create income streams.

The beauty of this approach is that it preserves the land itself while converting the land's productivity into caregiving funds.

Key takeaway: A working farm is like a milk cow—you can keep her and milk her, rather than selling her for beef.

Strategy 8: When Selling Is the Right Answer

Sometimes, despite your best planning, selling part of the farm is the smartest move.

Before you recoil at the thought, consider: selling 40 acres you never farmed anyway to fund 10 years of quality care for your spouse might be the most loving thing you can do. Keeping 160 acres intact for the next generation is better than losing all 200 acres to creditors or Medicaid estate recovery.

If you must sell:

- Sell the least productive or most geographically separated parcels first
- Consider installment sales to spread out capital gains tax
- Explore conservation easements that can reduce tax burden
- Time sales strategically (maybe sell in a low-income year to minimize tax)

- Use 1031 exchanges if you're trading land for other investment property

Selling isn't failure. Sometimes it's wisdom.

Key takeaway: A tactical retreat that preserves most of the farm is better than a last stand that loses everything.

Putting It All Together

Most farm families won't use just one of these strategies—they'll use several in sequence.

Year 1-2: Use income from operations and maybe some savings **Year 3-4:** Tap long-term care insurance or VA benefits **Year 5-7:** Transition to Medicaid while protecting exempt farm assets **If needed:** Sell a non-essential parcel or use life insurance cash value

The key is planning the sequence before you need it. Once you're in crisis mode, your options narrow.

Work with advisors who understand all these tools and can help you create a comprehensive funding strategy. The attorney who handles Medicaid planning may not know about VA benefits. The financial advisor who manages your investments may not understand caregiver agreements. You need a team.

Key takeaway: Funding care is like managing a drought—you use multiple water sources, you conserve where you can, and you plan ahead because waiting until the well runs dry is too late.

In the next chapter, we'll tackle the tax issues that can make or break your planning. Because it's not just about having money for care—it's about keeping as much of it as possible out of the government's pocket.

Chapter 5: Protecting the Land: Estate Planning Strategies for Multi-Generational Farms

Your grandfather paid $200 an acre for the home place in 1952. Today it's worth $12,000 an acre.

That appreciation is wonderful—until you realize what it means for your family when you die or when you need to move assets around for Medicaid planning or care funding.

Estate planning for farm families isn't about avoiding death—it's about avoiding the death of the farm itself.

The Multi-Generational Challenge

Most businesses have a simple succession plan: sell the business, divide the cash, everyone's happy.

But you can't split 400 acres five ways without destroying what made it valuable. You can't liquidate the farm without liquidating the lifestyle, the identity, and the legacy that came with it.

And you can't transfer farm assets without running headlong into three massive obstacles: estate taxes, capital gains taxes, and family dynamics.

Let's tackle them one at a time.

Understanding Estate Tax (And Why Most Farms Are Safe)

First, the good news: most farm families won't pay federal estate tax.

The One Big Beautiful Bill Act (OBBBA Act) locked in federal estate tax exemptions in 2026 at $15.00 million per person, or $30.00 million for a married couple. That's the total value of everything you own—land, equipment, life insurance, retirement accounts, the works—before the IRS takes a bite. The OBBBA Act also includes an annual inflation adjustment starting in 2027.

If your farm is worth $5 million, you're not paying federal estate tax. Even if it's worth $10 million, with proper planning between spouses, you're likely clear.

But: Some states have their own estate or inheritance taxes with much lower exemptions.

And: Estate tax exemption amounts don't matter if you need to qualify for Medicaid, which has much stricter asset limits (typically $2,000 in countable assets). Estate planning protects assets from the IRS. Medicaid planning protects them from being spent on care.

You need strategies for both.

Key takeaway: Estate tax is like a drought—some years it threatens you, other years it doesn't, but you always need to plan for it.

The Capital Gains Tax Time Bomb

Here's where things get painful for farm families.

Let's say your parents bought land for $100,000 that's now worth $1 million. If they sell it, they pay capital gains tax on $900,000 in gains—roughly $180,000 to the IRS (at 20% federal plus state taxes).

But if they hold it until death and pass it to you, you get a "step-up in basis." Your starting point for future tax calculations becomes the $1 million value at their death, not the $100,000 they paid. If you later sell for $1 million, you pay zero capital gains tax.

This step-up in basis is one of the most valuable tax benefits in the code. It's why farmers hold onto land instead of selling.

The problem: When you're planning for Medicaid or dealing with dementia, you might need to move assets around. Gifts to children, transfers to trusts, or asset sales can all trigger capital gains taxes or eliminate the step-up in basis.

The strategy: *Structure transfers to preserve the step-up whenever possible. Use tools like:*

Grantor Retained Annuity Trusts (GRATs): You transfer assets to a trust, receive payments for a set term, and at the end the assets pass to your heirs. If you outlive the term, the assets leave your estate with minimal gift tax. The assets remain in your estate for income tax purposes, so heirs still get the step-up.

Qualified Personal Residence Trusts (QPRTs): Similar to GRATs but specifically for your home/farmhouse. You transfer the residence to a trust, live there for a set term, then it passes to heirs at a reduced estate tax value.

Intentionally Defective Grantor Trusts (IDGTs): You sell assets to a trust in exchange for a promissory note. The sale removes future appreciation from your estate, but because it's a "grantor trust" for income tax purposes, you don't recognize capital gains on the sale and heirs eventually get a step-up.

These tools are complex and need expert guidance. But for farms worth several million dollars, the tax savings can be enormous—easily $200,000 to $500,000 or more.

Key takeaway: Capital gains tax is like compaction in your soil—it's invisible but it'll crush your yield if you ignore it.

The Life Estate: A Simple Tool That Protects the Farm

One of the most effective strategies for farm families is also one of the simplest: the life estate.

Here's how it works: You deed the farm to your children but retain a "life estate"—the right to live on and use the property for the rest of your life. The children own the property (technically called a "remainder interest"), but can't force you out or sell without your consent.

Why this works:

- You've transferred ownership, starting the Medicaid five-year clock
- You still control the property during your lifetime
- You can continue farming or collect lease income
- The property may be protected from Medicaid estate recovery after you die

- Your children get a step-up in basis at your death (yes, even though they already own it)

The downside:

- You lose the ability to sell or mortgage the property without your children's consent
- If a child gets divorced, creditor problems, or dies, their ownership interest could be affected
- You're trusting your children not to turn on you (rare, but it happens)

For farm families with good relationships and children who are committed to keeping the *farm, life estates are simple, effective, and relatively inexpensive to set up.*

Key takeaway: A life estate is like building a barn with your kids—you're still using it, but you've passed the ownership papers to the next generation.

Family Limited Partnerships and LLCs

For larger farms or families with complicated dynamics, a family limited partnership (FLP) or limited liability company (LLC) can provide more control and flexibility.

Here's the structure: The farm assets go into the FLP or LLC. You (the parents) own the general partner or manager interest (typically 1-2% of value) and most of the limited partner/member interests. You gift limited partner interests to your children over time.

Why this works:

- You maintain control through your general partner/manager position
- Gifted interests can be valued at a discount (20-40%) because they're minority interests with no control—so you can transfer more value without gift tax
- The structure provides liability protection for the farm
- You can specify restrictions on who can become an owner (preventing in-laws from getting control)
- Income can be distributed tax-efficiently to family members in lower brackets

The complexity: These structures must be legitimate business entities, not just tax dodges. You need:

- Proper documentation (operating agreements, partnership agreements)
- Regular meetings and record-keeping
- Business purposes beyond tax savings
- Arm's-length transactions between the entity and family members

FLPs and LLCs typically cost $5,000-15,000 to set up properly and require ongoing maintenance. For farms worth $3 million or more, the tax savings usually justify the cost and complexity.

Key takeaway: An FLP or LLC is like an irrigation system—expensive to install, requires maintenance, but makes everything run more efficiently.

The Charitable Remainder Trust: When You Want to Give Back

If you're charitably inclined and need income, a Charitable Remainder Trust (CRT) can be a win-win.

How it works: You transfer highly appreciated land to a CRT. The trust sells the land (tax-free because it's a charity). The trust pays you income for life or a set term of years. When you die, what's left goes to the charity you named.

Why farmers use this:

- No capital gains tax on the sale (the trust is tax-exempt)
- You get a charitable deduction now for the future gift to charity
- You receive income for life

- You remove the asset from your estate
- You're supporting a cause you care about

The catch: The land eventually goes to charity, not your kids. This works for land your children don't want to farm, or when you have more land than they need.

I've seen farm families use CRTs for non-contiguous parcels, parcels that were rented out anyway, or land that was more valuable for development than farming. They kept the productive home farm for the kids and used the outlying land to fund retirement and support charity.

Key takeaway: A CRT is like selling a piece of equipment you weren't using and putting the proceeds to work for you and your community.

Conservation Easements: Protecting Land and Reducing Taxes

If your goal is to keep the farm as farmland forever, conservation easements can provide significant tax benefits while ensuring the land never gets subdivided or developed.

How it works: You donate a conservation easement to a land trust or government agency. The easement restricts future development (no subdividing into housing tracts) but allows continued agricultural use. You retain ownership and can farm, sell, or pass the land to heirs—but they're bound by the same restrictions.

Tax benefits:

- Charitable deduction for the value of the easement (typically 30-60% of land value)
- Reduced estate tax liability (the land is worth less because it's restricted)
- Possible property tax reductions at the local level

Why farmers do this: Many farm families would never develop their land anyway. They want it to stay a farm. The easement formalizes that wish and generates tax benefits for doing what you planned to do anyway.

The considerations:

- The easement is permanent—your grandchildren will still be bound by it
- The easement must be donated to a qualified organization
- The IRS scrutinizes these heavily, so documentation must be solid
- You need a qualified appraisal of the easement value

For farm families passionate about land conservation and facing significant estate taxes, easements can save hundreds of thousands in taxes while ensuring the farm stays a farm.

Key takeaway: A conservation easement is like dedicating your land to agriculture permanently—and getting paid by the government to do it.

Dealing with the Non-Farming Heirs

This is where estate planning gets emotionally complicated.

You have four kids. One farms with you. Three don't. How do you leave the farm to the farmer without the other three feeling cheated?

Option 1: Equal isn't always fair. Leave the farm to the farming child and other assets (life insurance, retirement accounts, investment property) to the non-farming children. The values might not be exactly equal, but they're reasonable.

Option 2: Buy-sell agreements. The farming child gets the option to buy out their siblings at a predetermined formula (often a discount from market value). The siblings get cash, the farmer gets the farm.

Option 3: The family rent-back. The non-farming children inherit ownership interests, but they must rent to the farming sibling at a fair rate. Everyone benefits from the land's value, but the farmer controls operations.

Option 4: The long-term payout. The farming child inherits the farm but pays their siblings over 10-20 years. It's essentially seller financing from the estate.

Option 5: Life insurance equalizer. The farming child inherits the farm. The non-farming children are the beneficiaries of life insurance equal to the farm's value. Everyone gets equivalent value.

None of these options is perfect. But all of them are better than leaving everything equally to all children and forcing a sale or creating a dysfunctional co-ownership.

Have the conversation now. Let the non-farming kids express their feelings. Maybe they don't want the farm anyway—they just want to know you value them equally. Maybe they'd prefer a clean split now rather than fighting over it after you're gone.

Key takeaway: Fair doesn't always mean equal. Sometimes the kindest thing you can do is make the hard decisions yourself rather than leaving them for your kids to fight over.

The Role of Life Insurance in Farm Estate Planning

Life insurance might seem disconnected from farm planning, but it's often the glue that holds everything together.

How farmers use life insurance:

Estate tax payment: If you expect to owe estate tax, life insurance provides the cash to pay it without selling land.

Equalizing inheritances: The farmer gets the farm, the other kids get the insurance.

Business continuation: If you die unexpectedly, insurance provides cash for operating expenses until the next generation gets established.

Buy-sell funding: If you have partners, insurance funds the buyout of a deceased partner's interest.

For farm families, permanent life insurance (whole life or universal life) often makes more sense than term insurance because:

- You don't know when you'll die, and term expires
- Cash value can be accessed for care or other needs

- Death benefit is guaranteed regardless of health changes

The strategy: Buy insurance while you're young and healthy. A 45-year-old farmer in good health might pay $8,000-12,000 per year for a $1 million permanent policy. That same farmer at age 65 with health issues might be uninsurable at any price.

Key takeaway: Life insurance is like keeping cash reserves for a bad crop year—you hope you don't need it, but when you do, nothing else will substitute.

Annual Gifting: The Slow and Steady Approach

The IRS lets you give $19,000 per year per recipient (2026 amount) without filing a gift tax return or using any of your lifetime exemption.

A married couple can give $38,000 per child per year. With four children, that's $152,000 in annual transfers.

Over 10 years, that's $1.52 million transferred tax-free.

Often, with the high costs of housing and dependent care, young adults could benefit from receiving gifts earlier in life, rather than waiting for a future inheritance. Partial gifts earlier in life can be used as IRA or Roth IRA contributions to provide decades of tax-deferred or tax-free compound growth, providing for financially secure future retirements.

For farm families, this might mean:

- Gifting LLC or partnership interests annually
- Transferring life insurance policies to children
- Funding trusts for grandchildren
- Making cash gifts that children use to buy equipment or land from you at fair market value

Annual gifting doesn't grab headlines like the fancy trusts, but it's available to everyone and it works.

The key is starting early. If you wait until you're 80 and in poor health, you've lost decades of gifting opportunities.

Key takeaway: Annual gifting is like applying fertilizer—a little bit every year adds up to a massive difference over time.

Pulling It All Together

Estate planning for farm families isn't about one magic tool. It's about layering strategies:

- Life estates or trusts to protect land from Medicaid
- LLCs or FLPs for control and tax-efficient gifting

- Conservation easements to reduce estate taxes while preserving agricultural use
- Life insurance to equalize inheritances and provide liquidity
- Annual gifting to gradually transfer wealth
- Clear communication with heirs about who gets what and why

The earlier you start, the more options you have. A 50-year-old farmer with a dementia diagnosis still has time to implement most of these strategies. An 80-year-old farmer in late-stage dementia has almost no planning options left.

Don't let fear of complexity or cost paralyze you. The cost of doing nothing is almost always higher than the cost of planning.

Key takeaway: Estate planning is like maintaining a farm—do a little every year and the place runs smoothly. Ignore it for decades and everything falls apart at once.

In the next chapter, we'll focus on the tax landmines that can blow up even good plans—and the strategies to avoid them. Because protecting the farm means protecting it from the IRS, too.

Chapter 6: Tax Landmines and Opportunities: Preserving Wealth Through the Transition

You wouldn't plant corn in a field you knew was full of unexploded ordnance. But that's exactly what many farm families do with their tax planning—they plow ahead without knowing where the bombs are buried.

Dementia planning triggers tax events. Asset transfers, trust creations, property sales, Medicaid qualifications—every one of them has tax implications. Get them wrong and the IRS can take a bigger bite out of your farm than any disease ever could.

Get them right and you can preserve hundreds of thousands of dollars for your family instead of sending it to Washington.

The Big Three Tax Traps

Three taxes threaten farm families more than any others: capital gains tax, estate tax, and income tax on retirement accounts. Let's defuse them one at a time.

Capital Gains: The Hidden Cost of Appreciation

Your family's greatest asset—land appreciation—is also your greatest tax liability.

When you sell land, equipment, or livestock that's appreciated in value, you pay capital gains tax on the difference between what you paid and what you sold it for.

Current rates (2025):

- 0% if your income is below $47,025 (single) or $94,050 (married)
- 15% for most people
- 20% if your income is above $518,900 (single) or $583,750 (married)
- Plus 3.8% Net Investment Income Tax if you're above certain thresholds
- Plus state capital gains tax (varies by state)

Bottom line: You could pay 25-30% of your gain to taxes.

For a farm family, this means: Sell $500,000 worth of land to pay for care, and $125,000-150,000 goes to taxes. You net $350,000-375,000. That's a year or two of memory care eaten by taxes.

Strategies to minimize capital gains:

Installment sales: Instead of selling land for a lump sum, sell it over time. You spread the gain (and the tax) over multiple years, potentially staying in lower tax brackets.

1031 exchanges: Sell the farm and buy another "like-kind" property within a specific timeframe. The gain is deferred. This works if you're transitioning from active farming to land ownership or moving to be closer to family.

Opportunity Zone investments: Invest capital gains in designated Opportunity Zones. You defer the tax and potentially reduce it if you hold the new investment long enough. Limited usefulness for farm families but worth exploring.

Die with it: Blunt but true. The step-up in basis at death eliminates capital gains tax entirely. If you can fund care without selling, that's often the best tax strategy.

Key takeaway: Capital gains tax is like losing 25-30% of your crop to shrink—avoid it when possible, minimize it when you can't.

Estate Tax: The Threat That's Bigger Than It Seems

Most farmers think, "I'm not rich enough to worry about estate tax."

Maybe. But maybe not.

The federal exemption is $15 million per person in 2026. The Big Beautiful Bill Act passed in July, 2025 makes the exemption permanent and begins adjusting for inflation starting in 2027. Twelve states however, have their own estate or inheritance taxes with much lower exemptions—sometimes as low as $1 million.

Here's what counts toward your estate:

- Land at current market value
- Equipment at current value
- Livestock
- Crops and grain in storage
- Life insurance death benefits you own
- Retirement accounts (IRAs, 401(k)s)
- Cash and investments
- Your share of any business interests

A farm family with 800 acres at $10,000/acre is sitting on $8 million in land alone. Add equipment, livestock, retirement accounts, and life insurance, and you're easily over $10 million.

If you're married, proper planning can protect $30 million (2026) using both spouses' exemptions. But only if you plan correctly.

The portability trap: When the first spouse dies, the surviving spouse can "port" or transfer the deceased spouse's unused exemption to themselves. But you have to file an estate tax return within nine months of death to claim it—even if no tax is owed.

I've seen surviving spouses lose millions in exemptions because nobody told them to file the return. They didn't owe tax, so they didn't file. Years later when they die, that first spouse's exemption is gone forever.

Strategies to minimize estate tax:

Lifetime gifting: Use your exemption while you're alive to transfer assets to the next generation. Every dollar you gift is a dollar that's not in your estate.

Irrevocable Life Insurance Trusts (ILITs): Life insurance you own counts toward your estate. Life insurance owned by an irrevocable trust doesn't. For a farmer with a $2 million policy, that's $2 million removed from the taxable estate.

Valuation discounts: Assets transferred to FLPs or LLCs can often be valued at a 20-40% discount for gift and estate tax purposes. You can transfer more value using less exemption.

Charitable planning: Assets left to charity aren't taxed. For farmers with more than enough land for their heirs, charitable strategies can reduce estate tax while supporting causes they care about.

Key takeaway: Estate tax is like a hailstorm—it doesn't threaten every year, but when it hits, it can destroy everything. Have insurance (a plan).

Income Tax on Retirement Accounts: The Ticking Time Bomb

That $800,000 in your IRA? The government hasn't taxed it yet. They will.

Traditional IRAs and 401(k)s are tax-deferred, not tax-free. When you (or your heirs) withdraw the money, it's taxed as ordinary income—potentially at rates up to 37% federal plus state taxes.

The SECURE Act changed everything: Before 2020, heirs could "stretch" inherited IRAs over their lifetimes, taking small distributions and keeping the account growing. Now, non-spouse heirs must empty the account within 10 years.

For a farming heir who inherits a $1 million IRA, that means adding $100,000 per year of taxable income for 10 years. If they're already earning $80,000 farming, they're suddenly in the 24-32% federal tax bracket. They might lose 30-40% of the IRA to taxes.

Strategies to minimize IRA taxes:

Roth conversions: Convert traditional IRA money to Roth IRA while you're alive. You pay taxes now (hopefully at lower rates), but the money grows tax-free forever and heirs withdraw it tax-free.

This works especially well in years when your income is low—maybe you had a bad crop year, or you're semi-retired and collecting Social Security but not farming income. Convert enough to fill up the lower tax brackets.

Qualified Charitable Distributions (QCDs): If you're over 70½, you can donate up to $105,000 per year (2024) directly from your IRA to charity. The distribution doesn't count as taxable income, and it satisfies your Required Minimum Distribution.

For farmers who are charitably inclined anyway, this is free money. You were going to give to church or the local scholarship fund—why not do it from the IRA and avoid the tax?

Leave the IRA to charity, other assets to heirs: Charities don't pay income tax. If you have $500,000 in IRA money and $500,000 in land, leave the IRA to charity and the land to your kids. The charity gets full value from the IRA, and your kids get the land with a step-up in basis.

Key takeaway: IRAs are like grain in storage—you've grown it, but you haven't sold it yet. Plan your liquidation strategy carefully to minimize spoilage (taxes).

The Medicaid Tax Trap

Here's a trap that catches farm families by surprise: Medicaid estate recovery.

When you die after receiving Medicaid benefits, the state can file a claim against your estate to recover what they paid for your care. In many states, this includes not just nursing home costs but all Medicaid-covered expenses.

What this means: You spend down your assets, qualify for Medicaid, receive care for five years, and then die. The state files a claim for $300,000 against your estate. Your farm—

the one you carefully protected during life—gets hit with a huge tax bill after death.

Protections:

- Your home (and in many states, the farm) is exempt during your lifetime if your spouse still lives there
- Transfers made more than five years before applying for Medicaid are protected
- Liens can't be placed while a spouse or disabled child survives you
- Some states have hardship exemptions

But this is complicated and varies significantly by state. You absolutely need an elder law attorney who knows your state's rules.

Key takeaway: Medicaid estate recovery is like a loan that comes due when you die. Plan for it or it'll drain the estate you worked so hard to protect.

Income Tax Basis Planning: The Strategy Nobody Talks About

Let's get technical for a moment because this matters.

When you inherit property, your basis (your starting point for calculating future capital gains) "steps up" to the fair market value at the date of death.

Example: Dad bought land for $1,000/acre in 1975. It's worth $10,000/acre when he dies in 2025. You inherit it with a stepped-up basis of $10,000/acre. If you sell immediately, you have zero capital gains tax.

This step-up is powerful. It erases a lifetime of appreciation and lets the next generation start fresh.

But here's what people miss: The step-up only applies to property in the deceased person's estate. Property in irrevocable trusts, property given away, property in joint ownership with non-spouses—these don't always get the step-up.

Planning strategy: If you're planning to transfer assets to children anyway, and if the assets have significant appreciation, consider whether it's better to:

1. **Transfer now and start the five-year Medicaid clock**, knowing the kids won't get a step-up in basis and might face capital gains tax when they eventually sell, OR

2. **Keep the assets in your estate**, plan to use other funding sources for care, and give your kids the benefit of the stepped-up basis

For rapidly appreciating land: Sometimes transferring now makes sense because the five-year wait for Medicaid protection is predictable, but continued appreciation is not. A farm worth $3 million today might be worth $5 million in ten years. The $2 million in additional appreciation after transfer doesn't go through your estate.

For stable or slow-growth assets: Sometimes keeping them in your estate makes sense so heirs get the step-up and don't pay capital gains tax.

There's no universal answer. It depends on your health, your care funding plan, land values in your area, and your state's Medicaid rules.

Key takeaway: Basis planning is like deciding when to sell your grain—timing matters, market conditions matter, and getting advice from experts matters.

Handling the Tax on Equipment and Livestock

Land gets all the attention, but equipment and livestock have tax implications too.

Depreciation recapture: When you sell equipment you've been depreciating, you pay ordinary income tax on the depreciation you claimed. If you bought a $200,000 combine and depreciated it down to $80,000, then sell it for $100,000, you pay tax on $20,000 as ordinary income (recapture) and potentially capital gains on any amount over $200,000.

Livestock: Raised livestock has zero basis if you're a cash-basis farmer. Sell a cow you raised, and all the proceeds are taxable income. Purchased breeding livestock gets depreciated and can create recapture income when sold.

Strategies:

- **Time asset sales in low-income years** to minimize tax rates
- **Trade equipment** rather than sell when possible to defer taxes
- **Consider Section 1031 exchanges** for qualified property
- **Bundle sales and purchases** to offset income

Most of these strategies require planning ahead. Calling your accountant in December and saying "I sold $100,000 worth of equipment this year, how do I avoid the tax?" is too late. The tax is already baked in.

Key takeaway: Equipment and livestock taxes are like maintenance costs—you can't eliminate them, but proper planning minimizes their impact.

The Self-Employment Tax Surprise

Here's a trap that catches farm families using caregiver agreements:

If you hire your daughter as a caregiver and pay her $30,000 per year, that's self-employment income to her. She pays income tax plus self-employment tax (15.3% for Social Security and Medicare).

On $30,000, that's roughly $4,600 in self-employment tax alone.

Solutions:

- Structure it as W-2 employment if possible (you pay employer taxes, but she avoids self-employment tax)
- Keep records showing it's caregiving, not farm labor, to potentially avoid agricultural employment taxes
- Factor the tax into the compensation rate

Nobody likes surprise taxes. Talk to your accountant before implementing caregiver agreements to understand the full tax picture.

Key takeaway: Self-employment tax is like the interest on a loan—you knew it was part of the deal, but it still hurts when you write the check.

State Taxes: The Variable Nobody Remembers

Everything we've discussed assumes you understand your state's rules. But state tax laws vary wildly:

- Some states have no income tax (Texas, Florida, Tennessee)
- Some states have no estate tax (most states)
- Some states tax retirement income, others don't
- Some states tax Social Security benefits
- Property tax rates vary by thousands of dollars per year

If you're considering relocating to be closer to family or moving to a care facility in another state, state taxes matter.

Example: Moving from South Dakota (no state income tax, no estate tax) to Minnesota (top rate 9.85% income tax, estate tax starting at $3 million) could cost you tens of thousands per year in taxes.

This doesn't mean don't move—family and care quality matter more than taxes. But know what you're walking into.

Key takeaway: State taxes are like microclimates—they vary dramatically across short distances and can affect which crops (strategies) work best.

Working with Your Tax Professional

You need a tax advisor who understands:

- Agricultural tax rules (special use valuation, like-kind exchanges, etc.)
- Elder law (Medicaid planning implications)
- Estate planning (basis step-up, trust taxation)
- Multi-year tax planning (not just preparing last year's return)

That's a rare combination. Many CPAs handle farm taxes well but don't understand Medicaid. Many elder law attorneys understand Medicaid but aren't tax experts.

Build a team. Get your CPA and your attorney talking to each other. Have them review plans together. The money you spend on coordination saves you multiples in avoided taxes and mistakes.

And start the relationship early. The CPA you hire in a panic when you need to file a guardianship accounting is not the person to trust with complex multi-year tax planning.

Key takeaway: Your tax team is like your equipment dealer—you want a relationship built over years, not just someone you call in emergencies.

The Annual Tax Review

Here's a practice that separates families who preserve wealth from families who lose it to taxes: the annual tax review.

Every November, before year-end, sit down with your CPA and review:

- Projected income for the year
- Potential tax-saving opportunities (Roth conversions, equipment purchases, charitable giving)
- Required Minimum Distributions from IRAs
- Estimated tax payments for next year

- Long-term planning needs

This one meeting can save you thousands every year. Without it, you're just reacting to last year's taxes instead of planning this year's strategy.

Key takeaway: An annual tax review is like soil testing—do it regularly and you'll know how to adjust your plan before problems develop.

In the next chapter, we'll tackle Medicare, Medicaid, and the insurance maze. Because funding care isn't just about having money—it's about understanding which programs pay for what, and how to maximize every dollar.

Chapter 7: Medicare, Medicaid, and the Farm: Navigating Healthcare Benefits Without Losing Everything

You've been paying into Social Security and Medicare your whole working life. Now it's time to collect.

Except it's not that simple.

Medicare covers some things but not others. Medicaid covers different things but has strict asset limits. And the intersection of dementia care, farm assets, and government benefits is about as clear as a mud puddle after a three-inch rain.

Let's wade through it together.

Medicare: What It Covers (And What It Doesn't)

Most Americans think Medicare covers long-term care. Most Americans are wrong.

What Medicare DOES cover:

- Doctor visits and hospital stays
- Short-term skilled nursing care (up to 100 days after a hospital stay)

- Home health care if you're homebound and need skilled care
- Hospice care
- Some medical equipment

What Medicare DOESN'T cover:

- Long-term care in nursing homes
- Memory care facilities
- Custodial care (help with bathing, dressing, eating)
- Full-time home care
- Most dementia-related care beyond medical treatment

Here's the disconnect: Dementia care is mostly custodial, not skilled. You don't need a nurse to help someone get dressed or remind them to eat. You need a caregiver. Medicare doesn't pay for caregivers.

The skilled nursing benefit: Medicare will pay for up to 100 days in a skilled nursing facility following a qualifying hospital stay (at least three days). Days 1-20 are fully covered. Days 21-100 require a copay (currently $204 per day in 2025).

For farm families, this means: If your spouse falls, breaks a hip, spends three days in the hospital, and then needs rehab in a nursing facility, Medicare helps. But once the skilled therapy is done, if they still need care because of dementia, Medicare stops paying.

Key takeaway: Medicare is like basic liability insurance on your truck—it covers emergencies and medical treatment, but it won't pay to rebuild after a total loss.

Medicaid: The Safety Net That Requires Strategy

Medicaid is the program that pays for long-term care. But it's means-tested—you have to be poor (or become poor) to qualify.

Basic eligibility requirements:

- You must need nursing home level care or qualify for a home and community-based waiver
- Your countable assets must be below $2,000 (in most states)
- Your income must be below certain limits (varies by state)

For most people, qualifying for Medicaid means spending down assets until you have almost nothing left.

For farm families, it's more complicated—and more hopeful—because of agricultural exemptions.

The Agricultural Property Exemption

This is the golden rule for farm families: **Property used in a trade or business is often exempt from Medicaid asset limits.**

That means:

- Land actively farmed (by you, your children, or a tenant farmer)
- Farm equipment being used
- Livestock
- Buildings used for agricultural purposes
- Even farm inventory and crops

The key word is "actively." If you've retired from farming, sold the equipment, and are just sitting on land waiting to sell it, that land may count as a non-exempt asset. But if your son has taken over operations, the land is being farmed, and it's legitimately a business, you've got a strong case for exemption.

State-by-state variation: Every state's Medicaid program is slightly different. Some states are generous with farm exemptions. Others scrutinize them carefully. You absolutely need an elder law attorney who knows your state's rules.

Documentation matters: Keep records showing:

- Tax returns showing farm income
- Lease agreements if land is rented
- Business entity documents (LLC, partnership agreements)
- Proof the farm is actively operated

The better your documentation, the stronger your case that the farm is exempt property.

Key takeaway: A working farm is like a homestead exemption for your land—but only if you can prove it's actually working.

The Five-Year Look-Back

Medicaid looks at every financial transaction you made in the five years before you apply. Gifts, below-market sales, transfers to trusts—all of it gets scrutinized.

What they're looking for: Transfers made to artificially impoverish yourself to qualify for benefits.

The penalty: If you gifted $100,000 to your daughter three years ago, Medicaid divides that amount by your state's average monthly cost of care (say, $10,000) and makes you ineligible for that many months (10 months in this example). During the penalty period, Medicaid won't pay, but you still need care. Where does the money come from? That's your problem.

Exceptions to look-back penalties:

- Transfers to a spouse (no penalty)
- Transfers to a blind or disabled child (no penalty)
- Transfers of your home to a child who lived there and provided care for at least two years (no penalty)
- Transfers for fair market value (selling land for what it's worth isn't penalized)

The strategy: If you know dementia is coming and you want to protect assets, make transfers NOW. A transfer made today won't affect Medicaid eligibility five years from now. A transfer made in a panic next year might disqualify you right when you need coverage.

Key takeaway: The five-year look-back is like planting a crop—you do it in spring because you want to harvest in fall. Plan now for needs five years away.

Spousal Protections

If one spouse needs nursing home care and the other is healthy, Medicaid has protections so the healthy spouse doesn't become destitute.

The community spouse (healthy spouse) can keep:

- The home (regardless of value)
- One vehicle
- Up to $157,920 in countable assets (2025, varies by state)
- All income in their own name
- Monthly income allowance from institutionalized spouse if needed

The institutionalized spouse can keep:

- $2,000 in countable assets (in most states)
- A small personal needs allowance (around $50-75/month)

- Income above this goes to the nursing home, minus certain deductions

What this means for farm families: The healthy spouse can continue living on the farm, collecting farm income, and managing operations. The farm itself (if exempt) doesn't count toward asset limits. The community spouse can have nearly $160,000 in savings plus the farm. That's often enough to maintain the operation and prepare for succession.

The strategic opportunity: Some families shift more assets to the healthy spouse before applying for Medicaid. Maybe the institutionalized spouse's IRA gets used for care first, preserving the healthy spouse's assets. Or jointly-owned accounts get retitled to the healthy spouse. These strategies require careful planning and legal advice, but they can preserve significantly more wealth.

Key takeaway: Spousal protections are like keeping seed corn for next year—Medicaid understands the healthy spouse needs resources to survive.

Medicaid and the Home

Your primary residence is exempt from Medicaid asset limits, but there's a catch: estate recovery.

When you die, if you received Medicaid benefits, the state can file a claim against your estate to recover what they paid. In many states, this includes putting a lien on your home.

Protections against estate recovery:

- No recovery while your spouse is alive
- No recovery while a minor or disabled child lives in the home
- Hardship exemptions in some states
- Some states don't pursue recovery against small estates

The farm wrinkle: If your home is on the farm property, estate recovery could threaten the farm itself—not just the house. This is why advance planning with trusts or strategic transfers is critical.

Strategies to protect the home/farm:

- Transfer to a trust more than five years before needing care
- Transfer to a child who lived there and provided care
- Use life estate deeds

- Ensure farm remains exempt business property, not just residence

Key takeaway: Your home is protected during life but may be at risk after death. Plan accordingly.

Medicare Advantage vs. Traditional Medicare

Most people on Medicare have a choice: Traditional Medicare (Parts A and B) plus a supplement, or Medicare Advantage (Part C).

Traditional Medicare:

- You can see any doctor who accepts Medicare
- Supplement policies cover most gaps
- Predictable costs
- No network restrictions

Medicare Advantage:

- Often lower premiums (sometimes $0)
- Includes drug coverage
- May include dental, vision, hearing

- But: Network restrictions, referral requirements, prior authorizations

For rural farm families, Traditional Medicare is usually better because:

- Fewer doctors in rural areas accept Advantage plans
- You may need to travel for specialists
- If you winter in another state, Traditional Medicare works everywhere

But compare your specific situation. The Medicare.gov plan comparison tool is actually pretty good.

Key takeaway: Medicare Advantage is like buying store brand feed—cheaper up front, but might not work as well when you need it most.

Medigap Policies: Filling the Gaps

If you choose Traditional Medicare, you'll want a Medigap (Medicare Supplement) policy. These policies pay what Medicare doesn't—copays, deductibles, coinsurance.

Plan G is usually the sweet spot: Covers almost everything except the Part B deductible ($257 in 2025).

Monthly premiums vary widely by state and insurer, typically $100-250/month.

The enrollment window matters: You have a six-month window when you turn 65 to buy Medigap without medical underwriting. Miss that window and you might not qualify due to health issues.

For farm families: If you're on spouse's insurance through a job and delay enrolling in Medicare Part B, make sure you know when your guaranteed-issue window starts. Get it wrong and you could be stuck without supplement coverage.

Key takeaway: Medigap is like crop insurance—you buy it before you need it, and hope you never do.

Long-Term Care Insurance and Medicaid

If you have long-term care insurance, it works with Medicaid in a specific sequence:

1. Use LTC insurance benefits first (typically 2-5 years of coverage)
2. When LTC insurance runs out, spend down assets to Medicaid limits
3. Apply for Medicaid

Having LTC insurance buys you time. It delays the need for Medicaid, which might give you enough runway to transfer assets (and wait out the five-year look-back) or fund care without touching farm assets.

Partnership policies: Some states have "partnership" LTC policies. For every dollar your policy pays, you can protect an additional dollar of assets and still qualify for Medicaid. If your policy pays $200,000 in benefits, you can keep $200,000 above the normal Medicaid asset limit.

Not all states offer this. Check yours.

Key takeaway: LTC insurance plus Medicaid is like having two fuel tanks—when one empties, you switch to the other.

The VA Aid and Attendance Benefit

We touched on this earlier, but it's worth repeating: Veterans benefits can provide significant assistance and don't have the same harsh asset limits as Medicaid.

Aid and Attendance provides:

- Up to $2,431/month for a veteran (2025)
- Up to $1,318/month for a surviving spouse

- Up to $2,893/month for a married couple

Asset limits are more generous than Medicaid: Around $155,000 in countable assets (excluding home and one vehicle) depending on your situation. And the VA uses your net worth formula, which is less restrictive.

Application timeline: 6-12 months, so apply early. Use a VA-accredited attorney or veterans service organization.

Key takeaway: VA benefits are like a crop subsidy—free money if you qualify, but the paperwork is miserable

Home and Community-Based Services (HCBS) Waivers

Medicaid isn't just for nursing homes. Many states offer HCBS waivers that pay for care in your home or community, letting you stay on the farm longer.

Services covered might include:

- Home health aides
- Adult day care
- Respite care for family caregivers
- Home modifications (ramps, grab bars)
- Personal care services

The catch: Most states have waiting lists for these programs, sometimes years long. And some waivers have stricter functional requirements than nursing home care.

For farm families, HCBS waivers are golden because they let you stay on the land while receiving Medicaid-funded care. The farm remains productive, the family stays together, and quality of life stays higher.

Apply early. Get on the waiting list now, before you need it.

Key takeaway: HCBS waivers are like getting a farmhand subsidized by the government—if you can get in line.

Navigating the Application Process

Applying for Medicaid is complex. You'll need:

- Five years of bank statements
- Tax returns
- Asset documentation (deeds, titles, account statements)
- Income verification (Social Security statements, pensions, farm income)
- Medical documentation of need for care

- Proof the farm is an active business (if claiming exemption)

Common mistakes that delay approval:

- Missing documentation
- Unexplained large withdrawals or transfers
- Claiming farm exemption without proof of active operations
- Incomplete financial disclosure
- Not understanding your state's specific rules

Timeline: Expect 30-90 days for approval, longer if there are complications.

Hire help: An elder law attorney who handles Medicaid applications can be worth their weight in soybeans. They know what documentation is needed, how to present farm exemptions, and how to navigate denials or appeals.

Key takeaway: The Medicaid application is like filing for farm program payments—complex, paperwork-heavy, and easier with professional help.

Planning Ahead: The Decision Tree

Here's how to think about healthcare coverage planning:

Before age 65:

- Consider long-term care insurance (if healthy enough to qualify)
- Make sure you have health insurance through retirement
- Plan when to start Social Security and Medicare

At age 65:

- Enroll in Medicare Parts A and B (unless delaying due to employer coverage)
- Choose Traditional Medicare + supplement, or Medicare Advantage
- Enroll in Part D (drug coverage)
- If you're a veteran, apply for VA benefits

After dementia diagnosis:

- Understand what Medicare covers (not much for dementia care)
- Trigger LTC insurance if you have it
- Start five-year clock on asset transfers if planning for Medicaid
- Apply for VA Aid and Attendance if eligible

- Get on HCBS waiver waiting lists

When care needs increase:

- Use private pay, LTC insurance, or VA benefits initially
- Plan Medicaid application timing (after five-year look-back expires)
- Work with elder law attorney to structure assets properly
- Ensure farm qualifies for business exemption

Key takeaway: Healthcare planning is like crop rotation—you need a multi-year strategy, not just a reaction to this year's conditions.

In the next chapter, we'll tackle succession planning—how to prepare the next generation to take over when dementia makes it impossible for you to run things yourself. Because planning for your care and planning for the farm's future aren't separate tasks; they're two sides of the same coin.

Chapter 8: Preparing the Next Generation: Succession Planning When Time Is Short

You planned to have this conversation "someday."

Someday when you were ready to slow down. Someday when the farm was paid off. Someday when the kids were older and more experienced.

Then came the diagnosis, and someday became today.

Succession planning under the pressure of dementia isn't ideal. But it's still possible. And it's still necessary.

The Two Realities of Farm Succession

There are two types of farm succession, and dementia forces you to confront both simultaneously:

Management succession: Who's going to run things day-to-day? Who makes the calls about planting, marketing, financing, and operations?

Ownership succession: Who's going to own the farm? How do assets transfer? What happens to land, equipment, and the business entity?

Most families plan to handle these gradually—shift management over 10 years, transfer ownership slowly, ease the next generation into responsibility.

Dementia doesn't give you 10 years. You might have two good years, maybe three. After that, decision-making becomes impaired, legal capacity becomes questionable, and training becomes impossible.

So you accelerate. You telescope a decade of transition into 2-3 years. It's not ideal, but it's reality.

Key takeaway: Succession planning with dementia is like harvesting early because of a frost warning—not perfect timing, but better than losing the crop entirely.

Assessing What You Have to Work With

Before you can plan succession, you need an honest assessment of your situation.

Your health: How far has the dementia progressed? Can you still teach, explain, and make decisions? Or are you already past the point where you can effectively train someone?

Your successor's readiness: Is there an obvious next-generation farmer? Are they working on the farm now? Do they have the knowledge, skills, and desire to take over?

The farm's complexity: Are you running a simple grain operation, or a diversified farm with livestock, custom work, and multiple enterprises? Simpler operations transfer easier.

Financial position: Is the farm profitable? Heavily indebted? Can it support two generations, or does the senior generation need to step aside for the next to survive?

Family dynamics: Do all the heirs agree on who should take over? Is there resentment, jealousy, or conflict?

Be brutally honest. Pretending your son is ready when he's not doesn't help anyone. Pretending your daughter wants the farm when she's stayed away for 20 years creates problems, not solutions.

Key takeaway: Succession planning starts with honest inventory—you can't fix problems you won't acknowledge.

The Crash Course: What the Next Generation Needs to Learn

If you've got 1-3 years before dementia seriously impairs your ability to teach, here's what the next generation absolutely needs to learn:

Financial management:

- Where accounts are and how to access them
- How to read financial statements and track cash flow
- How to manage operating loans and lines of credit
- Understanding of tax obligations and filing requirements
- Insurance policies and claims processes

Operational knowledge:

- Agronomic decisions (seed selection, fertility, pest management)
- Equipment operation and maintenance
- Marketing strategies and when to sell
- Vendor relationships and who to trust
- Government program enrollment and compliance

Legal and regulatory:

- Business structure and how it operates

- Lease agreements and tenant relationships
- Environmental regulations and compliance
- Labor laws if you have employees
- Zoning and land use restrictions

Relationships:

- Who's the banker and what's our history with them?
- Which attorney, accountant, and advisors do we use?
- How do we work with crop consultants, veterinarians, agronomists?
- What's our reputation in the community and with neighbors?

That's a lot. Most farm kids learn it gradually over 20 years. You're cramming it into 2-3.

The strategy: Prioritize the financial and relationship knowledge first. Your successor can learn agronomy from a consultant or neighbor. But if they don't know which bank holds the operating note or where the insurance policies are, everything falls apart.

Key takeaway: Teaching a successor under time pressure is like teaching someone to drive in heavy traffic—start with the essentials and build from there.

Formalizing the Transition

Informal handoffs don't work when dementia is involved. You need structure.

Step 1: Get them on the bank accounts Add your successor as a co-signer or authorized user on all business accounts. They need to be able to access money, pay bills, and manage cash flow when you can't.

Step 2: Update business structure documents If you operate as an LLC or partnership, amend the operating agreement to clarify succession. Name your successor as manager or general partner with authority to make decisions.

Step 3: Establish signing authority Your lender needs to know your successor can sign loan documents, negotiate terms, and make financial decisions. Update signature cards and loan documents now, while you're still mentally competent to do so.

Step 4: Transfer equipment titles gradually Start putting equipment in your successor's name. This removes assets from your estate, starts the five-year Medicaid clock, and gives your successor ownership of the tools they need.

Step 5: Create written procedures Document your standard operating procedures. When do you soil test? Which seed varieties work on which fields? How do you calibrate the sprayer? Where are equipment manuals stored?

Your successor won't remember everything you tell them. Written procedures become the instruction manual they reference when you're not available to ask.

Key takeaway: Formalizing succession is like putting up posts and wire—it creates structure that holds things together when pressure hits.

The Land Question

This is where succession gets emotional.

You want the farm to stay in the family. You want your farming child to have it. But you also want to be fair to the non-farming children.

There's no perfect answer, but here are approaches that work:

The long-term lease Give the farming child a 10-20 year lease on the land at a below-market rate. They get security and the ability to make long-term plans. The non-farming children retain ownership and eventually inherit. Everyone shares in the land's value appreciation.

The purchase option Farming child gets the right to purchase the land at a predetermined price (often a discount from market value). They can exercise this option over time as they build equity. Non-farming children get cash.

The life estate You transfer ownership to all children equally, but the farming child gets exclusive use rights during your lifetime (and sometimes theirs). Keeps the farm intact operationally while being "fair" on paper.

The family land trust All children own shares in a trust that holds the land. The farming child manages and operates, but major decisions (selling, development) require consent from all siblings. Keeps the farm together across generations.

The unequal distribution Farming child gets the farm at a discount. Non-farming children get other assets (retirement accounts, life insurance, investment property) to equalize values. Not perfectly equal but practically fair.

Whichever approach you choose, document it legally and explain it to all the children while you still can. Let them ask questions. Address concerns. Get buy-in.

Springing this on the non-farming kids at your funeral creates lawsuits and destroyed relationships.

Key takeaway: Land succession is like dividing up inheritance—fair doesn't always mean equal, and everyone needs to understand why.

When There's No Next-Generation Farmer

What if none of your kids want the farm? Or they're not capable of running it?

You have options:

Lease it Keep the land but lease operations to a neighbor or tenant farmer. Your family retains ownership and benefits from appreciation, but someone else farms it.

Hire a farm manager Bring in professional management. They run the operation for a fee or share of profits. You (or your trust) remain the owner.

Sell to a neighboring farmer Often the cleanest exit. You get market value, the buyer gets to expand their operation, and you're done. Use proceeds to fund care and leave liquid assets to heirs.

Conservation easement and long-term lease Place a conservation easement on the land (locks it into agricultural use forever), get the tax benefits, then lease to a farming operation. The land stays productive and agricultural even without family involvement.

Transition to passive investment Convert from active farming to land ownership. Keep the real estate, sell equipment and livestock, collect rent. Much easier to manage as dementia progresses.

Many farmers feel like selling or leasing to a non-family member is failure. It's not. It's acknowledging reality and making the best decision for your situation.

Better to sell to a good neighbor who'll take care of the land than to force it on a child who doesn't want it and will eventually sell it anyway—probably for less and after years of conflict.

Key takeaway: Sometimes the best succession plan is realizing farming ends with your generation and planning accordingly.

The Communication Challenge

The hardest part of succession isn't the legal documents or financial structures. It's the conversations.

What you need to say to the farming child:

- "This is what I expect from you."
- "Here's what I'm giving you, and why."
- "This is how I want the operation run."
- "These are the family members and advisors you can count on for help."
- "I'm proud of you, and I trust you to steward this land."

What you need to say to the non-farming children:

- "I love you all equally, but fair doesn't always mean equal."
- "The farm goes to your sibling because they've worked here for 20 years and farming is their life."
- "Here's what you're receiving to balance the inheritance."
- "I need you to support your sibling, not fight them over this."
- "The farm staying intact honors our family more than dividing it into pieces no one can use."

What you need to say to your spouse:

- "If something happens to me, here's how I want the transition to work."
- "Support our child's decisions about the farm, even if you would've done it differently."
- "Don't undermine their authority by second-guessing every decision."

- "But also don't completely check out—they need your emotional support and wisdom."

Have these conversations now, while you can still articulate your thoughts clearly. Record them if necessary. Write letters. Do a video.

Years from now, when you can't remember or communicate, these words will matter to your family.

Key takeaway: Succession communication is like leaving your descendants a good fence—they may not appreciate it today, but they'll be grateful for years to come.

The Backup Plan

Here's what nobody wants to talk about: What if your chosen successor can't do it?

What if they get sick, or die, or discover they hate farming and quit? What if the dementia progresses faster than expected and they're not ready?

You need a backup plan:

Name a backup manager: If your first-choice successor can't serve, who's next? Another family member? A farm manager? A neighbor?

Build in an exit strategy: Include provisions in your succession documents for selling the operation if it becomes necessary. Don't lock your family into farming if it's destroying them financially or emotionally.

Create support systems: Line up advisors who can guide a young or inexperienced successor. Name co-trustees or advisory board members who can provide wisdom.

Fund professional management: Set aside resources to hire a farm manager if needed. Maybe your successor can learn the business while a professional keeps operations running.

Hope you don't need the backup plan. But create it anyway.

Key takeaway: A backup succession plan is like keeping spare parts for your combine—you hope you never need them, but you'll be glad they're there.

Timeline for Succession

If you've been diagnosed with dementia and haven't started succession planning, here's a realistic timeline:

Months 1-3:

- Have the family conversations
- Assess successor readiness
- Begin shifting operational responsibility
- Add successor to bank accounts and legal documents

Months 4-9:

- Transfer knowledge intensively
- Document procedures and relationships
- Begin shifting ownership of equipment and other assets
- Establish successor's relationships with lenders, vendors, advisors

Months 10-18:

- Continue ownership transfers
- Let successor make more decisions independently
- Step into advisory role rather than management role
- Monitor and provide feedback while you still can

Months 19-24:

- Complete ownership transfers where possible
- Ensure all legal documents are in place
- Step back from day-to-day management
- Focus on big-picture guidance and emotional support

Beyond 24 months:

- Your role becomes increasingly limited by dementia
- Successor is now fully in charge
- You benefit from systems you put in place earlier
- Family and advisors provide support your successor needs

Two years seems short for a complete succession. It is. But it's often what you have. Use it wisely.

Key takeaway: Succession under dementia is a sprint, not a marathon. Two years of focused effort beats ten years of "we should probably start thinking about this."

In the next chapter, we'll talk about building and coordinating your care team—the professionals who'll help you navigate the medical, legal, and financial maze ahead. Because you can't do this alone, and you shouldn't try.

Chapter 9: Building Your Care Team: Coordinating Medical, Legal, and Financial Advisors

You didn't build your farm alone.

You had the equipment dealer who kept your machinery running. The agronomist who helped you solve soil problems. The veterinarian who taught you how to manage herd health. The banker who believed in you when times were tight.

Navigating dementia is no different. You need a team. And you need them to work together, not operating in silos.

Why Farm Families Resist Getting Help

Let's acknowledge the elephant in the barn: farmers hate asking for help.

You've spent your life being self-reliant. You fix things yourself. You figure things out. Calling in experts feels like admitting defeat.

And there's the cost. Every professional you hire is money out of pocket. When you're trying to preserve assets for care and legacy, writing checks to attorneys and advisors feels wasteful.

But here's the truth: **The cost of not having the right team is far higher than the cost of hiring them.**

One mistake in Medicaid planning can cost you $50,000 in lost benefits. One poorly structured asset transfer can trigger $30,000 in taxes. One missing legal document can force a $20,000 guardianship proceeding.

Professional advice isn't an expense. It's insurance.

Key takeaway: Professional advisors are like buying quality seed—pay a little more upfront, get a much better harvest.

The Core Team: Who You Need

At minimum, every farm family dealing with dementia needs these five professionals:

1. Elder Law Attorney

This is your quarterback. The person who coordinates legal strategy, prepares documents, handles Medicaid applications, and protects your interests.

What they do:

- Draft or update powers of attorney, healthcare directives, wills, trusts

- Structure asset transfers to protect the farm
- Navigate Medicaid applications and appeals
- Handle guardianship proceedings if needed
- Coordinate with other advisors on legal implications of planning

What to look for:

- Specialization in elder law (not just general practice)
- Experience with agricultural assets and Medicaid exemptions
- Knowledge of your state's specific rules
- Membership in National Academy of Elder Law Attorneys (NAELA)
- References from other farm families

Cost: Expect to pay $250-500 per hour, or flat fees of $3,000-8,000 for comprehensive estate planning. Medicaid applications might cost $3,000-6,000. It's not cheap, but it's worth it.

Key takeaway: Your elder law attorney is like your veterinarian—you need one who knows your operation, specializes in what you need, and is available when crisis hits.

2. Financial Advisor/Planner

This person helps you understand your financial position, create care funding strategies, and make informed decisions about assets.

What they do:

- Analyze your financial situation and care funding options
- Help structure investments and income streams
- Coordinate with attorney on tax-efficient planning
- Advise on insurance products and benefits
- Project long-term financial needs

What to look for:

- Certified Financial Planner (CFP) designation
- Experience with long-term care and dementia planning
- Understanding of agricultural assets and farm finances
- Fee-only compensation (not commission-based)
- Willingness to coordinate with your other advisors

Cost: Fee-only advisors might charge $150-400 per hour, or a flat fee of $2,000-5,000 for comprehensive planning. Some work on a percentage of assets under management (typically 0.5-1.5% annually).

Key takeaway: A financial advisor is like a crop consultant—they can see problems you miss and help you maximize your resources.

3. CPA/Tax Accountant

This person keeps you out of trouble with the IRS and minimizes the tax hit on all your planning moves.

What they do:

- Prepare tax returns (personal, business, trust, estate)
- Advise on tax implications of asset transfers
- Help structure transactions to minimize taxes
- Coordinate with attorney on estate and Medicaid planning
- Represent you in IRS matters if needed

What to look for:

- Experience with agricultural taxation
- Knowledge of estate and gift tax rules
- Understanding of how Medicaid planning affects taxes
- Proactive planning approach (not just preparing last year's return)
- CPA license and good standing

Cost: Tax preparation might run $500-2,000 annually depending on complexity. Tax planning and advisory services might be $150-300 per hour.

Key takeaway: Your CPA is like your soil scientist—they help you understand what's underneath so you can plan better for the future.

4. Geriatric Care Manager or Social Worker

This person helps navigate the healthcare system and coordinate care services.

What they do:

- Assess care needs and create care plans

- Research and vet home care agencies, adult day programs, memory care facilities
- Coordinate medical appointments and communicate with healthcare providers
- Connect you with community resources and support services
- Monitor care quality and intervene when problems arise
- Provide emotional support and guidance to family caregivers

What to look for:

- Certification as a geriatric care manager or licensed social worker
- Experience with dementia care
- Knowledge of local resources and providers
- Strong communication and advocacy skills
- A person with dementia trusts and responds to

Cost: $100-200 per hour, or monthly retainer packages of $500-2,000 depending on level of involvement.

Many farm families skip this one because they think they can manage care themselves. But a good geriatric care manager can save you hundreds of hours of research, stress, and mistakes. If you live hours away from your parents, this person is essential.

Key takeaway: A geriatric care manager is like hiring a custom operator—they have the specialized equipment and expertise to do what you can't do yourself

5. Primary Care Physician with Geriatric Experience

This is the medical anchor. The doctor who coordinates all healthcare, manages medications, and makes referrals to specialists.

What they do:

- Monitor dementia progression
- Manage comorbid conditions (diabetes, heart disease, etc.)
- Coordinate care among specialists
- Prescribe and adjust medications
- Complete paperwork for disability, Medicaid, long-term care insurance

- Have difficult conversations about prognosis and care options

What to look for:

- Experience with dementia patients
- Good communication skills (explains things clearly, listens well)
- Willingness to coordinate with family members
- Accessible when problems arise
- Geriatric medicine certification or significant experience

If your family doctor is a general practitioner who sees mostly young families, consider finding a geriatrician or internist who specializes in older adults.

Cost: Usually covered by Medicare/insurance, though you may pay copays and deductibles.

Key takeaway: Your primary care physician is like your seed dealer—they're the first point of contact who connects you to everything else you need.

The Extended Team

Beyond the core five, you might also need:

Neurologist or geriatric psychiatrist for specialized dementia care and medication management

Elder mediator if family conflict is preventing good planning and decision-making

Insurance agent specializing in long-term care to review policies and maximize benefits

VA benefits specialist if you're a veteran trying to navigate Aid and Attendance

Professional farm manager if the next generation needs help while they're learning

Guardianship attorney if capacity is lost before documents are in place

Trust officer or professional trustee if family members can't or shouldn't serve

You don't need all of these. But know they exist when specific needs arise.

Getting Your Team to Work Together

Here's where many families fail: they hire good professionals, but those professionals never talk to each other.

The attorney creates an estate plan without consulting the CPA about tax implications. The financial advisor recommends strategies without checking if they'll disqualify you for Medicaid. The geriatric care manager finds a memory care facility you can't afford because nobody told them your budget.

The result? Wasted money, conflicting advice, and plans that don't work.

Key takeaway: Building your full team is like assembling your equipment lineup—you don't need everything, but you need the right tools for your operation.

How to coordinate your team:

1. Authorize communication Give each advisor written permission to talk to the others. HIPAA and privacy laws prevent professionals from sharing information unless you specifically authorize it.

2. Share documents Make sure everyone has copies of relevant documents. Your CPA needs to see the trust. Your attorney needs to know about insurance policies. Your financial advisor should review the Medicaid application.

3. Schedule joint meetings For major decisions, get key advisors in the room (or on a call) together. A one-hour meeting with your attorney, CPA, and financial advisor can prevent months of back-and-forth and conflicting advice.

4. Name a coordinator Often your elder law attorney or financial advisor becomes the de facto coordinator. They're the hub who makes sure everyone else is aligned.

5. Regular updates When your situation changes—health deteriorates, care needs increase, asset values shift—update all your advisors. Don't assume they'll find out on their own.

Key takeaway: A coordinated team is like a well-timed planting crew—everyone knows their role, nobody's duplicating work, and the job gets done efficiently.

What to Ask When Hiring Advisors

Don't just hire the first name someone gives you. Interview potential advisors and ask:

About their experience:

- "How many farm families have you worked with on dementia planning?"
- "How familiar are you with agricultural asset exemptions for Medicaid?"
- "Can you give me an example of a case similar to ours?"

About their approach:

- "How do you coordinate with other advisors?"
- "What's your communication style and availability?"
- "How will you keep me informed as things progress?"

About costs:

- "What's your fee structure?"
- "What's a realistic estimate for my situation?"
- "Are there ways to reduce costs if budget is a concern?"

About outcomes:

- "What results can I realistically expect?"

- "What are the risks or downsides of your recommended approach?"
- "What happens if things don't go as planned?"

Trust your gut. If an advisor talks down to you, dismisses your concerns, or pushes strategies you don't understand, find someone else.

Key takeaway: Hiring advisors is like buying equipment—ask questions, understand what you're getting, and don't buy from someone you don't trust.

The DIY Trap

Some families try to do everything themselves. They download forms from the internet, follow advice from Facebook groups, or wing it based on what worked for their neighbor.

Sometimes it works out. Often it doesn't.

The problems with DIY:

- One-size-fits-all documents don't account for farm-specific issues
- You don't know what you don't know (the mistakes you make are the ones you never see coming)

- Fixing mistakes costs far more than preventing them
- Government programs like Medicaid scrutinize DIY applications heavily
- You can't represent yourself in legal proceedings if you lack capacity

There's a middle ground: educate yourself (like you're doing with this book), but hire professionals for the technical execution. You wouldn't perform surgery on your own livestock—don't perform legal surgery on your estate.

Key takeaway: DIY planning is like building your own combine—theoretically possible, but the professionals have tools and expertise you don't.

When to Fire Your Advisors

Not every advisor relationship works out. Sometimes you need to make a change.

Warning signs:

- They don't return calls or emails promptly
- They can't explain strategies in terms you understand

- They push products or strategies that benefit them more than you
- They dismiss your concerns or don't listen
- They don't coordinate with your other advisors
- Your gut says something's wrong

Don't stay with an advisor out of loyalty or fear of offending them. This is your family's future. Demand competence, communication, and respect.

Key takeaway: Firing an advisor is like trading in equipment that doesn't work—it feels wasteful, but keeping broken tools costs you more in the long run.

The Caregiver as Team Member

Don't forget: the family member providing day-to-day care is also part of the team.

That might be a spouse, adult child, sibling, or other family member. They're not a professional, but they're on the front lines. They see what's working and what's not. They know the person with dementia better than anyone.

Include the caregiver in planning discussions:

- They understand current care needs and how they're changing
- They can report on what strategies are working
- They know the person's preferences and values
- They can flag when professional advice doesn't match reality

Support the caregiver:

- Acknowledge the burden they're carrying
- Provide respite care so they don't burn out
- Listen when they say they need help
- Don't second-guess their daily decisions from a distance

Family caregivers often know what needs to happen but feel guilty asking for help or spending money. The professional team should validate the caregiver's instincts and give them permission to use resources.

Key takeaway: The family caregiver is like your lead farmhand—they do the daily work that keeps everything running, and they deserve respect and support.

Building the Team When Money Is Tight

Professional advice costs money. If budgets are tight, prioritize like this:

Must have:

- Elder law attorney (for core documents and Medicaid planning)
- CPA (for tax compliance and planning)

Should have:

- Financial advisor (to create funding strategy and coordinate planning)

Nice to have:

- Geriatric care manager (if you're overwhelmed or live far away)
- Additional specialists as specific needs arise

Cost-saving strategies:

- Use legal clinics or reduced-fee services if available in your area

- Ask about flat fees instead of hourly billing
- Get the initial planning done, then maintain it yourself with occasional check-ins
- Use the elder law attorney for Medicaid but a general estate attorney for simpler documents
- Lean on non-profit resources (Area Agencies on Aging, Alzheimer's Association)

But be strategic about savings. Spending $5,000 on an attorney who protects $500,000 in farm assets is a bargain. Saving $3,000 by doing it yourself and losing Medicaid eligibility is disaster.

Key takeaway: Budgeting for advisors is like budgeting for inputs—buy what you truly need, but don't be penny-wise and pound-foolish.

In the next chapter, we'll bring everything together with a 12-month action plan. Because knowing what to do is worthless unless you actually do it. Let's map out exactly how to move from crisis to confidence.

Chapter 10: From Crisis to Confidence: Your 12-Month Action Plan

You've read nine chapters. You understand the challenges. You know the strategies. You're aware of the resources.

Now it's time to do something about it.

This chapter is different from the others. It's not information—it's implementation. It's your roadmap from where you are today to where you need to be twelve months from now.

Think of it as your planting and harvest schedule for protecting your family's future.

Month 1: Emergency Preparedness

Your first month is about stopping the bleeding and preventing immediate crises.

Week 1-2: Legal Documents

- ☐ Schedule appointment with elder law attorney (don't wait for an opening 6 weeks away—find someone available now)

- ☐ Gather existing legal documents: wills, trusts, powers of attorney, healthcare directives
- ☐ Make list of who you'd want to serve as agents and trustees
- ☐ Begin drafting/updating durable power of attorney for finances
- ☐ Begin drafting/updating healthcare power of attorney
- ☐ Complete advance directive/living will

Week 2-3: Financial Inventory

- ☐ List all bank accounts with current balances
- ☐ List all investment and retirement accounts
- ☐ Gather loan documents and balances
- ☐ Compile insurance policies (health, life, long-term care, farm)
- ☐ Locate deeds and titles for property and equipment
- ☐ Get copy of last 3 years' tax returns
- ☐ Create spreadsheet with assets, liabilities, income, expenses

Week 3-4: Medical Foundation

- ☐ Schedule appointment with primary care physician to discuss diagnosis and prognosis
- ☐ Request copies of all medical records related to dementia
- ☐ Ask doctor to complete any necessary disability or care certification forms

- ☐ Research specialists (neurologists, geriatric psychiatrists) if needed
- ☐ Understand your Medicare/insurance coverage

Week 4: Family Communication

- ☐ Schedule family meeting with spouse and adult children
- ☐ Prepare what you want to say in advance
- ☐ Have honest conversation about diagnosis, prognosis, and planning
- ☐ Begin discussing roles and responsibilities
- ☐ Don't try to solve everything—just start the dialogue

Goal for Month 1: Legal documents in place or in progress, financial picture clear, medical support identified, family aware and engaged.

Key takeaway: Month 1 is like spring field prep—you're not planting yet, but you're getting everything ready so you can plant when conditions are right.

Month 2: Professional Team Assembly

Now that immediate crises are addressed, build your advisory team.

Week 1: Attorney Finalization

- ☐ Finalize and sign all legal documents
- ☐ Ensure original documents are stored safely
- ☐ Provide copies to agents, financial institutions, healthcare providers
- ☐ Discuss Medicaid planning timeline with attorney
- ☐ Ask attorney for referrals to other professionals you need

Week 2: Financial Advisory

- ☐ Interview 2-3 financial advisors
- ☐ Choose one and schedule comprehensive planning session
- ☐ Provide financial inventory you created in Month 1
- ☐ Discuss care funding strategies and long-term projections
- ☐ Begin implementing recommended changes

Week 3: Tax Planning

- ☐ Meet with CPA to discuss tax implications of diagnosis and planning
- ☐ Review tax returns for planning opportunities
- ☐ Discuss timing of asset transfers and income recognition
- ☐ Create multi-year tax strategy
- ☐ Schedule follow-up meeting for year-end planning

Week 4: Care Coordination

- ☐ Research geriatric care managers or social workers in your area
- ☐ Interview and select one if you need this service
- ☐ Begin research on care options (home care, adult day care, memory care facilities)
- ☐ If applicable, apply for VA benefits (this takes 6-12 months)
- ☐ Get on waiting lists for HCBS waivers

Goal for Month 2: Professional team in place, everyone has the information they need, initial strategies identified.

Key takeaway: Month 2 is like assembling your crew for harvest—you're getting the right people in the right positions before the work gets intense.

Month 3: Asset Protection Planning

With your team in place, start executing on asset protection.

Week 1: Trust and Entity Review

- ☐ Review current business structure (sole proprietor, LLC, partnership)
- ☐ Discuss whether changes are needed for Medicaid protection

- ☐ Consider whether irrevocable trusts make sense for your situation
- ☐ Begin implementation if attorney recommends structural changes
- ☐ Update operating agreements, partnership documents

Week 2: Insurance Analysis

- ☐ Review long-term care insurance policy if you have one
- ☐ Understand what's covered, benefit periods, elimination periods
- ☐ If you don't have LTC insurance, confirm you're not eligible at this point
- ☐ Review life insurance—consider whether cash value should be accessed
- ☐ Ensure all insurance beneficiary designations are current

Week 3: Property Transfers

- ☐ Discuss with attorney which assets should be transferred for Medicaid planning
- ☐ Begin the 5-year look-back clock on strategic transfers
- ☐ Consider life estates, joint ownership, or trust transfers
- ☐ Document the business purpose for any transfers
- ☐ File gift tax returns if applicable

Week 4: Farm Exemption Documentation

- ☐ Gather evidence that farm is actively operated
- ☐ Ensure tax returns show farm income
- ☐ Document lease agreements if land is rented
- ☐ Take photos of active operations
- ☐ Create file with all documentation proving business activity

Goal for Month 3: Asset protection strategy implemented, Medicaid five-year clock started where appropriate, documentation in place.

Key takeaway: Month 3 is like treating your fields—you're applying what you need now so it works when you need it later.

Month 4-6: Succession Planning Foundation

Months 4-6 are about transferring knowledge and formalizing succession.

Month 4 Tasks:

- ☐ Have formal conversation with farming successor about expectations

- ☐ Add successor to business bank accounts as co-signer
- ☐ Update signature authority with lenders
- ☐ Begin intensive knowledge transfer (daily operations, financial management)
- ☐ Create written procedures for critical tasks
- ☐ Introduce successor to key vendors, advisors, and lenders

Month 5 Tasks:

- ☐ Begin shifting operational decision-making to successor
- ☐ Let successor manage more of the financial operations
- ☐ Document relationships and contacts
- ☐ Start transferring equipment titles if part of succession plan
- ☐ Have difficult conversations about non-farming heirs and inheritance
- ☐ Continue knowledge transfer

Month 6 Tasks:

- ☐ Successor should be managing most day-to-day operations now
- ☐ Your role shifts to advisor and oversight
- ☐ Update business documents to reflect succession changes

- ☐ Discuss long-term land transfer strategy with attorney and family
- ☐ Begin implementing chosen succession strategy
- ☐ Document everything in writing

Goal for Months 4-6: Successor operating farm with increasing independence, formal succession plan in motion, family aligned.

Key takeaway: Months 4-6 are your growing season—you've planted, now you're cultivating and watching growth happen.

Month 7-9: Care Planning and Resource Maximization

Mid-year focus shifts to care planning and maximizing benefits.

Month 7 Tasks:

- ☐ Complete care needs assessment with geriatric care manager or social worker
- ☐ Tour memory care facilities in your area (even if not needed yet)
- ☐ Interview home care agencies
- ☐ Research adult day programs

- ☐ Create cost estimates for different levels of care
- ☐ Begin implementing respite care for primary caregiver

Month 8 Tasks:

- ☐ File for LTC insurance benefits if you have a policy
- ☐ Follow up on VA benefits application (if applicable)
- ☐ Check status of HCBS waiver applications
- ☐ Review Medicare coverage and consider supplement changes for next year
- ☐ Implement caregiver agreement if family member is providing care
- ☐ Begin tracking care expenses for tax deductions

Month 9 Tasks:

- ☐ Meet with financial advisor to review care funding progress
- ☐ Adjust strategies based on disease progression and care costs
- ☐ Consider whether Roth conversions make sense this tax year
- ☐ Review asset protection plan with attorney—is anything time-sensitive?
- ☐ Complete any needed property transfers before year-end
- ☐ Join dementia support groups (both for person with dementia and caregiver)

Goal for Months 7-9: Care plan in place, benefits maximized, funding strategy being implemented, support systems engaged.

Key takeaway: Months 7-9 are like mid-season adjustments—you're addressing problems, optimizing systems, and preparing for what's ahead.

Month 10-12: Year-End Planning and Looking Ahead

Final quarter is about tax planning, reviewing progress, and preparing for the next year.

Month 10 Tasks:

- ☐ Schedule year-end tax planning meeting with CPA
- ☐ Review income and deductions for the year
- ☐ Make any needed income adjustments or equipment purchases
- ☐ Complete annual gifting to children if part of strategy
- ☐ Review estate plan—any updates needed?
- ☐ Assess disease progression—is timeline matching expectations?

Month 11 Tasks:

- ☐ Review insurance coverage for next year
- ☐ Make Medicare plan changes during open enrollment if needed
- ☐ Ensure all legal documents are up to date and accessible
- ☐ Update financial inventory
- ☐ Review succession plan—is it working as intended?
- ☐ Address any family conflicts or communication issues

Month 12 Tasks:

- ☐ Schedule annual meetings with all advisors for next year
- ☐ Review and document everything accomplished this year
- ☐ Identify what still needs to be done
- ☐ Create action plan for Year 2
- ☐ Celebrate progress—you've done hard work
- ☐ Rest and recharge before the next year's efforts

Goal for Months 10-12: Tax optimization completed, progress reviewed, plan for Year 2 created, family positioned for success.

Key takeaway: Months 10-12 are harvest and storage—you're gathering what you've grown and preparing for the next season.

Beyond Year 1: The Ongoing Journey

Your 12-month plan isn't a finish line. It's establishing the foundation for ongoing management.

Year 2 priorities typically include:

- Continuing asset transfers if on Medicaid planning timeline
- Completing succession transition
- Adapting care plan as disease progresses
- Reviewing and updating strategies as circumstances change
- Maintaining relationships with advisory team

Year 3-5 priorities often shift to:

- Potentially applying for Medicaid (if five-year look-back period complete)
- Transitioning to higher levels of care
- Managing estate and inheritance issues
- Supporting the next generation in their new roles

The work doesn't end, but it becomes more manageable because you've built the systems, relationships, and knowledge to handle whatever comes.

What Success Looks Like

Twelve months from now, if you've followed this plan, here's what should be true:

✓ All legal documents in place protecting your interests

✓ Assets structured to maximize Medicaid protection

✓ Professional advisory team assembled and coordinating

✓ Farm succession plan implemented and working

✓ Care funding strategy established and being executed

✓ Family communication improved and conflicts addressed

✓ Benefits (VA, LTC insurance, etc.) activated

✓ Tax strategy optimized

✓ Care plan in place matching disease progression

✓ Primary caregiver supported and not burning out

You won't have everything perfect. Dementia throws curveballs. But you'll have transformed from crisis mode to confident management of a difficult situation.

Key takeaway: Success isn't eliminating all problems—it's having the tools, team, and plan to handle problems as they arise.

The "I'm Overwhelmed" Version

Maybe you're reading this thinking, "There's no way I can do all of that."

Fair enough. Here's the stripped-down version focusing only on what's absolutely critical:

Months 1-2: Must-Do List

1. Get durable power of attorney for finances (attorney)
2. Get healthcare power of attorney (attorney)
3. Complete advance directive (attorney or do yourself)
4. Create financial inventory (do yourself)
5. Have family conversation (do yourself)

Months 3-4: Must-Do List 6. Meet with elder law attorney about Medicaid planning 7. Meet with CPA about tax implications 8. Begin one strategic asset transfer to start 5-year clock 9. Add successor to farm bank accounts 10. Apply for VA benefits if eligible

Months 5-12: Must-Do List 11. Transfer key knowledge to successor 12. Set up caregiver agreement if family providing care 13. File for LTC insurance benefits if you have policy 14. Create succession plan for the farm 15. Review everything with advisors before year-end

That's 15 items over 12 months. Roughly one task every 3 weeks. Much more manageable, and it covers the most critical ground.

Key takeaway: Don't let the perfect be the enemy of the good. Do what you can, when you can, and keep moving forward.

When Things Don't Go According to Plan

They won't. Dementia progresses unpredictably. Family conflicts arise. Financial situations change. Legal rules shift.

When the plan needs adjusting:

If disease progresses faster than expected: Accelerate succession and asset transfers. Focus on crisis management over optimization. Get successor fully in charge sooner.

If disease progresses slower than expected: Use the extra time for more thorough planning. Complete additional asset protection strategies. Invest more in training the successor.

If financial situation worsens: Prioritize immediate needs over long-term protection. Consider selling non-critical assets. Adjust care plans to lower-cost options.

If family conflict erupts: Bring in professional mediator. Don't let disagreements paralyze all planning. Make decisions with or without consensus if necessary.

If key successor can't fulfill role: Activate backup plan. Consider professional farm management. Explore selling or leasing the farm.

The plan is your guide, not your prison. Adapt as needed.

Key takeaway: A plan that adapts to changing conditions is better than a perfect plan that can't bend without breaking.

Final Thoughts: From Crisis to Confidence

A year ago—or maybe a week ago—you got the diagnosis. It felt like the ground disappearing beneath your feet.

Today, or twelve months from today, the diagnosis is still there. Dementia hasn't gone away. The challenges remain.

But you've transformed how you face them.

You've moved from reactive panic to proactive planning.

From isolation to a team of professionals supporting you.

From fear about the future to confidence that you've done everything possible to protect your family and farm.

You've given your farming successor the tools to continue your legacy.

You've structured assets to preserve as much as possible for the next generation.

You've ensured your spouse won't be destitute.

You've documented your wishes so your family knows what you want.

You've created systems that will continue working even when you can't manage them yourself.

That's not failure. That's stewardship. That's love. That's what farmers do--we plan, we adapt, we work hard, we protect what matters, and we pass it on to the next generation in better shape than we found it.

The land has taught you everything you need for this journey: patience, resilience, adaptability, the importance of preparation, and the wisdom of asking for help when the job's too big to handle alone.

You've weathered droughts and floods, good markets and bad, equipment breakdowns and crop failures. You've figured out a thousand problems that seemed unsolvable.

You can do this too.

Not perfectly. Not without hard days. Not without losses.

But you can do it. And twelve months from now, you'll look back and realize you already have.

Key takeaway: Confidence doesn't come from having all the answers. It comes from having a plan, a team, and the determination to keep putting one foot in front of the other.

Appendix: Your Action Tracker

Make a copy of this tracker and check off tasks as you complete them. Don't worry about doing everything perfectly or in exact order. Progress matters more than perfection.

Month 1:

- ☐ Elder law attorney appointment scheduled
- ☐ Existing legal documents gathered
- ☐ Financial inventory completed
- ☐ Family conversation held
- ☐ Medical appointments scheduled

Month 2:

- ☐ Legal documents signed
- ☐ Financial advisor selected
- ☐ CPA meeting completed
- ☐ Care coordinator identified if needed
- ☐ Team has all necessary information

Month 3:

- ☐ Asset protection strategy decided
- ☐ Strategic transfers initiated
- ☐ Farm exemption documentation created
- ☐ Insurance policies reviewed

- ☐ Beneficiaries updated

Months 4-6:

- ☐ Successor added to accounts
- ☐ Knowledge transfer plan created
- ☐ Written procedures documented
- ☐ Succession conversation with family held
- ☐ Operational handoff progressing

Months 7-9:

- ☐ Care needs assessed
- ☐ Care options researched
- ☐ Benefits applications filed
- ☐ Caregiver agreement implemented
- ☐ Support systems engaged

Months 10-12:

- ☐ Year-end tax planning completed
- ☐ Insurance coverage reviewed
- ☐ Progress evaluated
- ☐ Next year's plan created
- ☐ Advisory team meetings scheduled

You've got this. One month at a time. One task at a time. One day at a time. Let's get to work.

Endnotes and References

This section provides citations for the statistics and research referenced throughout the book. While this book is designed to provide practical guidance rather than academic analysis, we believe it's important to ground our recommendations in reliable data.

Chapter 1: When the Diagnosis Comes to the Farm

Dementia Incidence in General Population

1. **42% of Americans over age 55 will develop dementia**
    - Source: Rush Alzheimer's Disease Center, Rush University Medical Center
    - Note: This statistic represents lifetime risk for individuals aged 55 and older based on longitudinal studies of aging populations.

Dementia Risk in Agricultural Workers

2. **Agricultural workers have 46% greater odds of developing dementia**
    - Source: Multiple occupational health studies examining dementia risk across professions

- Research has documented elevated dementia risk among agricultural workers compared to other occupational groups, with factors including pesticide exposure, noise-induced hearing loss, and higher rates of depression contributing to increased risk.

3. **Pesticide exposure linked to cognitive decline**
   - Source: Agricultural Health Study and other occupational exposure research
   - Studies have shown associations between chronic exposure to organophosphate and organochloride pesticides and lasting toxic effects on the central nervous system.

4. **Depression doubles dementia risk and occurs at higher rates among farmers**
   - Source: Multiple epidemiological studies on mental health in agricultural populations
   - Research documents that depression is associated with approximately twofold increased risk of developing dementia, and farmers experience higher rates of depression due to factors including isolation,

financial pressures, long work hours, and pesticide exposure.

5. **Noise-induced hearing loss as dementia risk factor**
    - Source: Audiology and cognitive health research
    - Hearing loss is recognized as a major modifiable risk factor for dementia, and agricultural workers have higher rates of noise-induced hearing loss from farm equipment exposure.

Cost of Dementia Care

6. **Total cost of dementia care in the United States: $781 billion (2025)**
    - Source: Alzheimer's Association, 2025 Alzheimer's Disease Facts and Figures
    - This figure represents the total annual costs of health care, long-term care, and hospice care for people with dementia.
7. **Unpaid care by families and friends: $247 billion**
    - Source: Alzheimer's Association, 2025 Alzheimer's Disease Facts and Figures

- This represents the estimated value of unpaid caregiving provided by family members and friends, calculated based on caregiving hours and market rates for equivalent services.

8. **Average annual cost per person with dementia: over $53,000**
    - Source: Alzheimer's Association cost analysis
    - This figure includes direct medical costs, long-term care expenses, and other dementia-related expenditures, though actual costs vary significantly based on disease stage and care setting.
9. **Lifetime costs can exceed $321,000**
    - Source: Alzheimer's Association and health economics research
    - Lifetime cost estimates vary based on age at diagnosis, disease progression rate, type of care received, and geographic location. This figure represents median estimates for comprehensive dementia care from diagnosis through end of life.

10. **Average duration from diagnosis: 4-8 years**

- Source: Multiple longitudinal dementia studies
- Disease duration varies significantly by dementia type, age at diagnosis, and individual factors. Some individuals live 20+ years after diagnosis, while others progress more rapidly.

Additional Resources and Data Sources

Government and Public Health Organizations

- **Centers for Disease Control and Prevention (CDC)**
  - Provides data on dementia prevalence, risk factors, and public health initiatives
  - Website: www.cdc.gov/aging/dementia
- **National Institute on Aging (NIA)**
  - Conducts and supports research on Alzheimer's disease and related dementias
  - Website: www.nia.nih.gov
- **Administration for Community Living**
  - Oversees programs supporting older adults and people with disabilities
  - Website: acl.gov

Alzheimer's and Dementia Organizations

- **Alzheimer's Association**
    - Leading voluntary health organization in Alzheimer's care, support, and research
    - Publishes annual "Alzheimer's Disease Facts and Figures" report
    - 24/7 Helpline: 800-272-3900
    - Website: www.alz.org
- **Alzheimer's Foundation of America**
    - Provides support, services, and education for individuals and families affected by dementia
    - Website: www.alzfdn.org

Agricultural Health and Safety

- **Agricultural Health Study**
    - Prospective study of pesticide applicators and their spouses in Iowa and North Carolina
    - Examines relationships between agricultural exposures and health outcomes
    - Website: aghealth.nih.gov
- **National Institute for Occupational Safety and Health (NIOSH)**

- Conducts research and makes recommendations for prevention of work-related injury and illness, including in agriculture
- Website: www.cdc.gov/niosh/agriculture

Legal and Financial Planning Resources

- **National Academy of Elder Law Attorneys (NAELA)**
  - Professional association for attorneys specializing in elder law
  - Attorney referral service available
  - Website: www.naela.org
- **U.S. Department of Veterans Affairs**
  - Information on Aid and Attendance benefits and other veteran services
  - Website: www.va.gov
- **Centers for Medicare & Medicaid Services**
  - Official information on Medicare, Medicaid, and related programs

    - Website: www.cms.gov and www.medicare.gov

State-Specific Resources

Many of the legal and financial strategies discussed in this book vary by state. For state-specific information:

- Contact your state's Area Agency on Aging
- Consult your state's Medicaid website for eligibility rules and exemptions
- Check with your state bar association's elder law section
- Review your state's department of agriculture for farm-specific programs

Disclaimers

The statistics cited in this book represent the best available data at the time of publication. However, readers should be aware:

1. **Dementia risk factors and incidence rates** continue to be studied, and understanding evolves as research progresses.
2. **Cost estimates** vary significantly based on geographic location, type of care received, and individual circumstances. The figures provided represent national averages or medians.
3. **Agricultural exemptions and Medicaid rules** differ substantially by state. Always consult with an elder law attorney licensed in your state for guidance specific to your situation.
4. **Tax laws and benefit programs** change regularly. The information in this book reflects laws and programs as of the publication date.
5. **Individual experiences** with dementia vary widely. Progression rates, symptoms, and care needs differ from person to person.

Important Disclaimer

This book is designed to provide general information and guidance for agricultural families facing dementia. It is not intended as:

- Legal advice for your specific situation
- Financial advice tailored to your circumstances
- Medical advice or diagnosis
- Tax advice for your particular case
- A substitute for professional counsel

Every family's situation is unique. The strategies discussed in this book may or may not be appropriate for your circumstances. Always consult with qualified professionals—including elder law attorneys, financial advisors, CPAs, and healthcare providers—before making significant legal, financial, or medical decisions.

The author and publisher make no representations or warranties regarding the accuracy, completeness, or timeliness of the information contained in this book. Laws, regulations, and best practices change over time. Readers are encouraged to verify current information with appropriate professionals and authorities.

Updates and Corrections

For updates to information in this book, additional resources, or to report errors, please visit https://www.s2wealth.com or contact Keith Piscitello at keith.piscitello@s2wealth.com

---

Final Key Takeaway: The strength of agricultural families lies not just in the land they tend, but in their willingness to seek knowledge, ask for help, and plan for the future. May this book serve as a trusted companion on your journey.

Made in the USA
Coppell, TX
14 March 2026

73639977R20105